SAMUEL BUTLER: A CHRONICLE
AND AN INTRODUCTION

BERNARD SHAW: A CHRONICLE AND AN INTRODUCTION

By R. F. RATTRAY

Cloth, 5s. net

" Dr. Rattray's painstaking little book could be described as a Handbook to G. B. S. . . . His knowledge of Mr. Shaw's writings and the books that have been written about the master and his works is immense. Future generations may regard this book as a First Primer to the man and his works."—*The Sunday Times*.

" His book is valuable. It is exactly what it is said to be. The students of Shavian literature will be grateful for it."—MR. ST. JOHN ERVINE in *The Observer*.

" It is my business to emphasize the importance of this book. . . . Articles and plays are illustrated and criticized while the man and his thought mature before our eyes."—*Western Mail*.

" Should prove of invaluable assistance to students of the subject . . . admirable both for its truthfulness and for handiness of consultation."—*Glasgow Herald*.

SAMUEL BUTLER: A CHRONICLE AND AN INTRODUCTION

by

R. F. RATTRAY

DUCKWORTH
3 Henrietta Street, London, W.C.2

First Published in 1935
All Rights Reserved

Made and Printed in Great Britain by the KEMP HALL PRESS, LTD.
in the City of Oxford

ACKNOWLEDGMENTS

WHOSOEVER reads about Butler and, much more, whosoever writes about him, must be deeply indebted to the late Mr. Festing Jones. His labours in the biography are well known. I have the additional debt to him that he showed me the outstanding kindness that was characteristic of him, corresponded with me regularly, and was very grateful and encouraging when I was able to render any little service to the propagation of Butler's writings. I am confident that he would have as graciously given me permission to make the fullest use of the writings of Butler and himself as would the late Mr. A. T. Bartholomew, who showed me favours similar to those of Jones, and as have in fact the present owners of the copyright, Mr. Geoffrey Keynes and Mr. Brian Hill, and the publishers of Butler's books, Messrs. Jonathan Cape. To all of them I am deeply grateful.

The Times has most obligingly given me permission to quote from the article, " Samuel Butler as Sheep Farmer," published in the issue for September 10, 1932, and from a leading article entitled " Simplicity," which appeared in the issue for December 18, 1923.

Acknowledgments to other sources are made by references in the text and footnotes.

26 Queen Edith's Way,
 Cambridge.

Mr. Bernard Shaw wrote of Samuel Butler in his preface to *Major Barbara*, in 1906, as being " in his own department the greatest English writer of the latter half of the nineteenth century. It drives one almost to despair of English literature," he went on to say, " when one sees so extraordinary a study of English life as Butler's posthumous *Way of All Flesh* making so little impression. . . . Really, the English do not deserve to have great men."

Wherein does Butler's claim to recognition consist ? The first answer is, in originality and depth. Sir Grafton Elliot Smith has said that the inertia of tradition and public opinion and the lack of courage to defy them when evidence fails to conform to them, seem to be potent to blind all but the ablest and most fearless of men to facts which are really patent. Butler was sensitive to such facts in a way that ought to be normal but is at the opposite pole from being average. He was a man of deeply sensitive feeling : this emerged in deep passions, but there was latent in him titanic strength which was largely used in controlling himself and pretending to be unmoved. The records of Butler reveal a heart hungry to love and be loved.

From his childhood, he was thwarted by father, mother, sisters and all the people whom convention represented to be sympathetic. He was ready to acquiesce in the ways of the world, but conscientiousness made it clear to him that the ways of the world—many of the most approved ways of the world—were contrary to the truth. He came to be Zoroastrian in his worship of the truth and his hatred of the lie, but he was always unflinching in avoiding the attitude of the prig. This constant struggle between two positions apparently opposed constitutes the chief difficulty in the way of his being understood.

It has been truly pointed out that genius is simply this sensitiveness to truth in experience : it is simply eminent ability : the form in which it finds expression is not necessarily dictated to be any particular one. It was really by historical accident that Shakespeare was a dramatist, Newton a scientist, and Wren an architect. In Butler's case the eminent ability came out in great versatility. His first significant interest was in the truth in religion. Then his originality enabled him to criticize life with the insight of genius, and thus he is chiefly known as a satirist. But really his greatest contribution is in the philosophy of evolution. Darwin had produced what Shaw has described as " the revelation of a method by which all the appearances of intelligent design in the universe may have been produced by pure accident." Butler, by one of the *aperçus* of genius, saw that, as conscious will can become unconscious, it can extend back through evolution *ad infinitum*. He wrote some half-dozen whole books to elucidate this subject alone.

Once Butler realized that convention, however august, is no guarantee of truth, he became definitely sceptical of the conventions, and proceeded to work for substitutes for those that, on examination, he found to be untrue. This, combined with his artistic nature, led him to translate the Iliad and the Odyssey into contemporaneous English instead of the jargon conventionally approved for the purpose. This in itself was a task of years, especially as his conscientiousness led him to commit the whole of both works to memory—although, to his chagrin, he discovered that he could retain only a few books of them at a time. Then in reading the Odyssey he saw conventional classical scholarship fall in ruins in the discovery that the poem was written by a girl. This had to be followed up and demonstrated. Then if Homer had been thus mishandled, what about Shakespeare? What about the problem of the sonnets? More industry and another book.

By this time we have a picture of a crank, a man slightly insane, who has largely lost adjustment to " reality," whose egomania has led him to think that he knows better in whole fields of scholarship than the accumulated labours of generations of great scholars.

But it cannot be denied that rank outsiders have been proved to be right time after time to the confusion of the accumulated wisdom of generations of scholars. So it was with Schliemann. Nor can it be denied that some men have been incredibly versatile and incredibly successful in their versatility.

Few people realize what a powerful weapon is the single eye for the truth. Few indeed are those who do not succumb to some of the temptations of the world not to see or not to speak the truth in respect of some of the things the world professes to believe and does believe. The ideal witness would be a man who had absolute objectivity and yet had grown up inside the world criticized, so that he could understand it. Now, Butler escaped the temptations that corrupt all but the very few. Owing to his originality, he became alienated from his conventional family so that he was no longer affected in his work to any vital degree by family consideration. He had no itch for social recognition strong enough to induce him to conceal his truth for its sake. While having had an academic education, he emancipated himself entirely from its trammels. The need of economic subsistence, which shuts the mouths of many, was met in his case partly through his own attainments in the economic sphere and partly through inheritance—although he knew bitter economic uncertainty. Lastly, the consideration of professional opinion he was relieved of by the fact that he was a free lance.

Surely the fact ought to be grasped once and for all that genuine criticism implies the affirmation of positive values. So Butler was always pursuing real values. Music was the dominating passion of his life ; then the other arts—painting, in which he strove to be an executant, sculpture, literature. But always his main activity was criticism of life, revealed in his novel, his note-books and all his books. Viewed in this light, the way in which Butler lived becomes an inspiring epic. Book after book he laboriously wrote, could not find a publisher for, and published at his own expense. Book after book was received with contumely and did not sell. Yet he kept on, rich in humour, with deep confidence in the truth.

Not that Butler, even in his lifetime, was wholly a failure. The obituary notice in *The*

Press, New Zealand, said with much truth : " He painted—and his pictures were hung ' on the line ' at the Royal Academy. He composed—and competent critics declared his ' Narcissus ' not unworthy of Handel. . . . And all this while his one great popular success passed through edition after edition, and *Erewhon* has long since taken its place in English literature as the greatest book of its class since *Gulliver's Travels*."

Butler had of course faults, and some of them were very serious. He was highly sexed, and from youth believed himself incapable of sexual continence. Marriage as established appeared to him an unreasonable institution and he believed himself driven for sexual relief to prostitutes. In Butler's mind this took a logical form. He was not responsible for how he was made and this was the only way out that society provided. It is notorious that there has been no great man but has had a blind spot and in view of Butler's development otherwise, it is to me staggering that he did not see the selfishness in his conduct and strive to meet this issue more honourably.

Then there is his reaction against conventions that amounted almost to a mania. His improvised epidermis was naturally in some places too hard. Such violence was done to his nature by conventions and conventional people that he

became so suspicious of conventionally approved
persons that he developed, in the words of Shaw,
" some of the stigmata of the chained dog."
And yet, on another side of him, he acquiesced
rather too easily in convention.   No doubt some
of this was compensation : he who differs from
the world on important matters ought the more
carefully to comply with it in unimportant ;
but, for example, he grew up in the feudal system
still surviving in the nineteenth century and, as
Shaw has pointed out, acquired the attitude that
cannot allow human considerations wholly to
triumph over social stratification.   In other
words, although in many ways at the opposite
pole from snobbery, he was in some ways sub-
consciously a snob.   He had little or no interest
in economic reform.

Butler's suspicion of conventions passed into a
joke and almost into an obsession. Behind a lot
of this were—as is usual in such cases—a deep
intuitive knowledge of his own worth and jealousy
of much inferior men who had won great reputations falsely, and his protest was not merely
selfish but was against injustice and mis-leading.
Sir William Phipson Beale, Q.C., a friend of his,
said, " People misunderstood Butler : he did not
want praise, he wanted sympathy," and with this
Butler's greatest friend agreed.   But criticism of

conventions was carried on by Butler and his friends in a manner that sometimes degenerated into the freemasonry of the callow.

No one repented of his faults, real and imagined, more bitterly than did Butler when he became aware of them. A college friend, Canon McCormick, wrote of him, " I fancy he lived too much alone. We must not altogether judge him as we judge other men." He was very lonely. His painfully conscientious, and yet selfish, attachment to his friends reveals the pathos of his life. Out of his meagre resources he allowed £200 a year for many years to his friend Pauli—even, after a crisis in his economic affairs, paying it out of his meagre capital—although Pauli treated him with bitter unkindness. There is abundant testimony to his deep yet selfish affection, consideration for others, generosity, kindness. Much of his selfishness was due to his vocation for his work : he had to save himself in order that it, with all its great strain, should be done.

Butler had many, and many prolonged, devastating visitations upon his soul but in its secret shrine he ever kept undimmed the flame of the spirit. He had the good fortunes of his heroic enterprise—including a man friend and a woman friend and a servant friend who were all but ideal.

Butler was descended from yeoman stock of Warwickshire. His great-grandfather was a shopkeeper. His grandfather was Dr. Samuel Butler, Headmaster of Shrewsbury and later Bishop of Lichfield. When the latter went to Shrewsbury there was only one boarder : under him the school grew famous : he trained more distinguished scholars than any other man : he had considerable influence on the public school life of England—reforms credited to Arnold were really due to him—and therefore on the life in general of England.

Our Samuel's father was seventh in the Classical Tripos. He did not wish to enter the Church, he wished to enter the navy, but Dr. Butler decided on the former. He became an assistant master at Shrewsbury. He married a Miss Worsley, a member of a well known Bristol Unitarian family (she, however, became a devout Churchwoman). Later, Thomas Butler became Rector of Langar, near Nottingham. He was regarded by many, including members of his family circle, as a kind, and even playful man. He was an amateur botanist of some distinction. Late in life, he was made a Canon of Lincoln.

There was an interesting set of parallels between the families of the Butlers and the Darwins. Dr. Butler was Bishop of Lichfield ; Erasmus

Darwin lived in Lichfield. Erasmus Darwin's son, Dr. Robert Waring Darwin, was the leading medical man in Shrewsbury while Thomas Butler was a boy. The Darwins were Unitarians ; Samuel Butler's mother had been a Unitarian. Charles Darwin was a friend of Thomas Butler ; he it was who inoculated Thomas with his taste for botany ; and later Samuel was to come across Charles Darwin and his sons.

Samuel Butler was born at Langar on December 4, 1835. His father, mother and sisters were conventional according to Victorian types. They are set down, essentially, but not of course with truth in detail, in *The Way of All Flesh*. Butler's is a moving story. Here is a passage he wrote in *The Fair Haven* :

> All children love their fathers and mothers, if these last will only let them ; it is not a little unkindness that will kill so hardy a plant as the love of a child for its parents. Nature has allowed ample margin for many blunders, provided there be a genuine desire on the parent's part to make the child feel that he is loved, and that his natural feelings are respected. This is all the religious education that a child should have. As he grows older, he will then naturally turn to the waters of life, and thirst after them of his own accord,

by reason of the spiritual refreshment which they and they only can afford. Otherwise he will shrink from them, on account of the way in which he was led down to drink against his will, and perhaps with harshness, when all the analogies with which he was acquainted pointed in the direction of their being unpleasant and unwholesome. So soul-satisfying is family affection to a child that he who has once enjoyed it cannot bear to be deprived of the hope that he is possessed in Heaven of a parent who is like his earthly father—of a friend and counsellor who will never, never fail him.

As it is also written in *The Fair Haven*, the rottenness of still-born love in the heart of a child may poison the blood of the soul.

Butler's father is a sinister figure. No doubt he was a thwarted man himself, condemned to be a clergyman when his heart was not in it. As we have seen, he was regarded by many, including members of his family circle, as a kind, and even playful man. He has been defended by Mrs. Garnett, in her book, *Samuel Butler and his Family Relations*. But anyone who happens to have the gift of reading character from photographs can see in the photograph of Canon Butler reproduced in *Butleriana* a pigheaded, cruel man. Butler's mother became a mere process of her husband. She would invite the confidence of her small son and then betray him to his father, who thrashed him.

Samuel Butler's education began early. He has told of it in *The Way of All Flesh* :

Before [he] could well crawl he was taught to kneel ; before he could well speak he was taught to lisp the Lord's prayer and the general confession. How was it possible that these things could be taught too early ? If his attention flagged or his memory failed him, here was an ill weed which would grow apace unless it were plucked out immediately ; and the only way to pluck it out was to whip him or shut him up in a cupboard or dock him of some of his small pleasures of childhood. Before he was three years old he could read and, after a fashion, write. Before he was four he was learning Latin and could do rule-of-three sums.

Butler wrote at another time :

I began Latin when only a few months over four years old, and my father thrashed it into me (I mean physically) day after day for years. I have no recollection of anything else.

As a boy of eight Samuel was taken abroad travelling in Italy, with which he fell in love and which became to him his second motherland. At

that he more especially embodied and throughout their lives disliked all that reminded them of him. Such boys, however, were in a minority, the spirit of the place being distinctly Skinnerian.

"First hearing the music of Handel," says Butler's biographer, " was the second great event in Butler's life; and thenceforward Italy and Handel were present always with him as a double pedal to every thought, word and deed." It is remarkable that both in the case of Butler and of Shaw the dominant influence from childhood on their lives was music.

Butler as a boy developed some interest in drawing. At the age of eighteen he again visited Italy and deepened his impressions, including those of the art of the old masters. There is no doubt that an artistic bent in him was coming out, and here again it may be worthy of remark that the second greatest influence on Shaw also was pictorial art. For those who admire both writers it would appear that in education music and other art ought to have greater opportunity than they commonly do.

Butler went up to St. John's College, Cambridge. His rooms were in D New Court, top storey but one, and Second Court, groundfloor of staircase C, right of staircase. He read mathematics. At college again he was "up against" the compact or solid majority—even in its anarchy and he produced a satirical "Prospectus of the Great Split Society." He was opposed, too, to an Evangelical movement that was on in the college and wrote a skit on the kind of religious tract that was circulated. It was printed and contains evidence of the independence and originality and strength of mind that were characteristic of Butler.

There was a valuable property on the outskirts of Shrewsbury known as the Whitehall, in which by his grandfather's will, his aunt, Mrs. Lloyd, and his father had successive life interests and which was to come to Butler on his father's death as tenant in tail. In 1857, when he was at Cambridge, his aunt and father wanted to sell a portion of this property and got Butler to consent to this without any remuneration. He did not grasp that the land, which was then used only for grazing, would, by the time it came to him, be building land, and he gave his consent. The entail was cut off, the sale made, the entail was then put on again, and the remaining land plus the purchase money resettled on the original terms. Mrs. Lloyd and Canon Butler made a profit out of this, but Butler got nothing of it.

In 1857 Butler went on a Continental tour with a certain Joseph Green for three weeks. In 1858, Lent Term, an essay by Butler was published in the first number (Vol. I, No. 1) of the *Eagle*, a St. John's College magazine, "On English Composition and Other Matters." This contains some interesting and significant passages. Similes, he says, show the symmetry of the world's arrangement. A good book, to be read properly, nearly always requires *effort*. Originality is rare, but the only shame in borrowing from others is in not acknowledging. Good subjects for the artist are to hand, but it requires unusual intelligence to find them. The artist must not merely reproduce, he must improve. Young men ought not to write beyond their experience, but, on the other hand, there are some things in which experience blunts the mental vision: these things are better described by young men. "A man should be clear of his meaning before he endeavours to give it any kind of public utterance and, having made up his mind what to say, the less thought he takes how to say it, more than briefly, pointedly, and plainly, the better." From these principles Butler, although for long enough art was for him only a bye-work, never departed.

They were in fact revolutionary principles.

The accepted ones were very much in favour of the cultivation of " style." So late as Stevenson's well-known essay we have the status quo. It is true that Swift and Dr. Johnson had looked forward to the time when people would write in a straight-forward way, but at the end of the nineteenth century Butler and Shaw were in fact pioneering the new, natural way of writing which has insensibly asserted itself and is brought to our notice now only when we read the stilted " styles " of bygone times.

In an article describing his tour of 1857 which appeared in the *Eagle*, No. 5, Easter Term, 1859, Butler reveals here and there his strength of mind. He recognizes, for example, that a foreign town may appeal to one really by its unfamiliarity when one thinks it is by its beauty. A mode of expression which anticipates *Erewhon* is in reference to " Strasbourg, where we ascended the cathedral as far as they would let us without special permission from a power they call Mary."

Among the skits he wrote during his undergraduate time was one on examinations, a paper for shoeblacks—e.g., " Prove that the scraping-knife should never be a secant and the brush always tangent to the shoe."

Butler was a member of a " Republic Society "

at Upware. Among the members were H. A.
Morgan, afterwards Master of Jesus, James Clerk
Maxwell, A. R. Ward, cricketer, and the Rev.
T. G. Bonney.[1]

Butler, it will be remembered, was reading
mathematics, but within a year of his final he
changed to classics and nevertheless was
bracketed twelfth in the first class.

He then went to London and began to prepare
for ordination, living and working among the
poor. The discovery that some of the boys he
had to deal with had not been baptized and that
they were not evidently different from those who
had been," shook his faith," and he declined to
be ordained, and returned to Cambridge with a
view to taking up university teaching. He got
one or two private pupils and an odd job like
examining a school at Bolton. His father took
his deviation from the way to Holy Orders very
much amiss and there was a long and painful
correspondence—pathetic from the point of view
of Samuel. The latter really wanted to be an
artist; he was pursuing the study of art. The
correspondence of this time shows again his
remarkable maturity. There came " pain and

[1] *The Fenman's World*, quoted in *The Times Literary Supplement*,
1930, July 17.

estrangement, which was none the less profound for being mutually concealed."

Finally it was decided that he should go to New Zealand—to a Church of England colony—and take up sheep-farming. On the voyage thither he read Gibbon's *Decline and Fall of the Roman Empire*.[1]

Butler adapted himself amazingly well to the extraordinarily different conditions of life in which he found himself. He was for some time isolated in an upcountry ranch with elementary men whose language familiarized itself to him. His aesthetic and intellectual interests continued with unabated energy. So great was his love of music and his determination, that he had a piano brought up to his settlement, fording rivers on the way. Here he played Bach fugues and studied the New Testament critically.

In the Butler collection at St. John's College, Cambridge, are two copies of the New Testament in Greek of the same edition, one of 1851, and both containing numerous marginal notes by Butler. These notes belong to the Cambridge-New Zealand period. A comparison led me to the conclusion that the copy with the advertisements at the end was annotated later than the

---

[1] This made a deep impression on him. The irony in Gibbon's chapters on Christianity and his general style come out in Butler—notably in *The Fair Haven.*

other. In the former, notes read " our Lord,"
and the ending " -eth " in the third person
singular of the verb is generally used (" He
telleth " and the like), whereas in the notes in the
other copy the usual practice is to say simply
" he," and to use the ending " -s " for the
third person singular of the verb (" he goes "
and the like). In the second copy, opposite
I Timothy vi, 13 and following verses is the note
" A strong passage for Unitarians." In the first
copy, opposite I Timothy ii, 9 and following
verses is the note, " Precepts for women which I
would they would attend to," and in the second
copy is the note, " Women not to be expensively
clad and not to wear the b———s." Opposite I
Timothy ii, 15 is the note, " Women to be
saved by child-bearing (!) " He read other
literature as well and wrote notes.

In 1861, writing to a cousin who was a
Unitarian, Butler said:

I do not believe that there is a particle of
important difference between your creed and
mine; I utterly refuse to enter into minute
disquisitions concerning the nature of the
Trinity and damn all who differ from me;
and, without going so far as the Archbishop of
Constantinople, who affirmed the Athanasian
Creed to be the composition of a drunken man,

I will not hesitate to avow my belief that it deserves no more attention than if it were. . . .

Much as there is in Gibbon which we should alike condemn—for, however we may admire his sarcasms, it is impossible not at times to feel that he would have acted more nobly in suppressing them—he is a great historian and the impress of a mighty intellect is upon his work.

In a letter in the same year to a friend he wrote, " I think I am a Unitarian now, but don't know and won't say."

In 1860 or 1861 he read *The Origin of Species.* This is remarkable, for it will be remembered that the book was first published in 1859. He became an enthusiastic admirer of Darwin.

In *The Times* for September 10, 1932, appeared an interesting article about Butler, reproducing extracts from the diaries of Edward Chudleigh, an English public school boy who had arrived in New Zealand in 1861 and who frequently toiled up to Butler's settlement to help the latter with his work or to keep him company. He wrote:

Mr. Butler came here to-day he is one of the cleaverest men in N.Z. he is a little man and nearly as dark as a Mowray, and is at present very nearly if not quite an infidel, and yet I believe would not do a dishonourable

thing to save his life, he admires a man that
sticks to his belief no matter what it is.

In 1862 Butler came to the conclusion, as a
result of his studies in the New Testament, that
Jesus did not die upon the cross. He wrote
down his arguments for this view.

He wrote "Darwin on the Origin of Species:
A Dialogue." This was published in a newspaper called *The Press*, Canterbury, New Zealand,
in December, 1862. It excited a great deal of
interest in the colony. An article replying to it
was published in *The Press* entitled "Barrel-
Organs," the idea being that there was nothing
new in *The Origin of Species*; it was only a grinding-
out of old ideas. Butler replied and there was
further correspondence.

A copy of Butler's article came into the
hands of Charles Darwin, who sent it to an
English editor with the following note :

Mr. Darwin takes the liberty to send by this
post to the Editor a New Zealand newspaper
for the very improbable chance of the Editor
having some spare space to print a Dialogue
upon Species. This Dialogue, written by
someone quite unknown to Mr. Darwin, is
remarkable for its spirit, and from giving
so clear and accurate a view of Mr. D.'s
theory.

After a while Butler went to live in Christ-church, contenting himself with occasional visits to his station. Of this period a New Zealander wrote :

His friends here remember how, if a mis-chance befel him, or the world went awry with him, he would sit down at his piano and pour out his anger in a burst of passionate music or give vent to his grief in a wailing minor till the mood passed; or, if good news came to him, his exultation found voice in the same way and he would sit for hours at the keys improvising glad melody.[1]

Butler met Charles Paine Pauli, who was to play an important part in his life. He was a Winchester and Oxford man. Butler looked up to him as " everything I should like myself to be, but knew very well I was not." Butler, his biographer tells us, was always nervous and diffident about his own manners and appearance unless he was interested in the company or the conversation and then he forgot everything else. Pauli took everyone by storm. Butler became devoted to him with a dog-like devotion.

According to Chudleigh, already quoted—at Mr. Tripp's station-house Mrs. Tripp (Bishop Harper's daughter) found his " peculiar and wild

[1] *The Press*, New Zealand, 1902, July 28, obituary notice.

theories upsetting " and did not like it when Butler tried to " convert the maid to his ideas." But " he played the piano beautifully and would do so for hours."

Butler wrote a letter to the editor of *The Press*, which was published among the correspondence, headed " Darwin among the Machines."

Butler's letters home describing his life in New Zealand, put together, were sunk in a shipwreck and later were fished up from the wreck and were edited and published by his father as a little book, *A First Year in Canterbury Settlement*, in 1863.

In 1864 a tiny volume was published at Christchurch, printed at *The Times* office, entitled *Literary Foundlings*. Among the collaborators was Butler, who contributed a " Note on *The Tempest*, Act III, Sc. i." The passage referred to is the speech of Miranda:

> My father
> Is hard at study; pray now rest yourself;
> He's safe for these three hours.

On this Butler comments: " Safe. If she had only said that 'papa was safe' the sentence would have been purely modern and have suited Thackeray as well as Shakespeare. See how quickly she has learnt to regard her father as one to be watched and probably kept in good humour for the sake of Ferdinand."

Chudleigh wrote in his diary for March 19, 1864:

Had a long talk with Butler on various subjects, I think he is gone as far as man can go now, he is an ultra-Darwinian, he thinks Darwin in 200 years hence will be looked upon as a most wonderful philosopher, and possibly a prophet, he does not believe the Bible to have been written by men under the influence of divine inspiration, but by *good men*, he thinks it a book, for all social and moral purposes, full of moral truths, and a book to be followed. I think he does believe in an almighty something, somewhere; he does not believe there is a colossal etherial being, that pervades all space and matter, whose person would pass through the densest matter as unconscious of resistance as a feather in a vacuum, he thinks the time will come when man, a very different being to the present worm, will look back on us much in the same light as we look on the Silurian Epoch, the names of all the great men that influence the world will be forgotten but their influence will be handed on from age to age, modified and infinitely improved, just as we feel the influence of the first invention of the lever, wheel and pulley. Give the World time, an infinite number of epochs, and according to its past and present system, like the coming tide each epoch will advance on each, but so slowly that it can barely be traced, man's body becoming finer to bear his finer mind, till man becomes not only an Angel but an Archangel.

Here he said, My dear boy you are quite right to maintain your own opinions, but you cannot blame me for doing as I do, holding such opinions. I shall not do it (a thing I had been talking to him about) because I do not think it right, I do right because I think it wrong to do otherwise. "Right" is that which agrees with the law and interest of man, and I suppose, human instinct is to tell one right from wrong. This point I do not quite comprehend. I have not used his language but these are some of his views.

Butler had prospered. "My sheep had bred; wool had kept high and so had sheep; runs which were pretty cheap when I reached New Zealand had gone up greatly in value. I had got hold of mine bit by bit and had pieced it into a compact, large, well bounded, and in all respects desirable property; but I was heavily involved with my merchants; I saw that if things fell—

c

as they presently did—I might easily be cornered.
I felt moreover that the life was utterly uncon-
genial to me and I thought it wiser to sell and go
home, leaving my money at 10 per cent., which
was the rate of interest then current." Butler
was then twenty-seven.

His affairs took some months to settle and
Pauli and he were constantly together. Pauli
wanted to go home and qualify for the bar. As
Butler wrote later: "I believed myself worth not
less than £800 a year. What could be simpler
than for me to say I would lend him £100 to
take him home and (say) £200 a year for three
years till he could get called and go out to New
Zealand again? He was to repay me when he
came into his reversion, and if more was wanted,
his father and mother might be relied upon to
do it."

They came home on a sailing vessel of 400
tons. They arrived in London in the autumn of
1864 and by September were settled in Clifford's
Inn, Fleet Street, in two sets of chambers which
Pauli found. The set occupied by Pauli was
rented at £12 per annum. The set occupied by
Butler was at No. 15, on the second floor, and
consisted of a sitting-room, a bedroom, a painting-
room, a pantry and a passage with cupboards in
it. The rent was £23. Water was not laid on and

had to be fetched from below in the court.   An old woman came in the morning to clean up, make his bed, etc.   Butler lived here all the rest of his life.

He began to attend Cary's art school.   But he continued to write a little.   He sent an article entitled " Lucubratio Ebria " to *The Press*, New Zealand, and it was published in that journal in July, 1865.   It reveals profound philosophical insight.   Butler sketches the whole theory of the gradual building up of the human mind through all the stages of evolution.   He makes observations which were to be characteristic of his thought—e.g., " We know that what we see is but a sort of intellectual Siamese twins, of which one is substance and the other shadow, but we cannot set either free without killing both."

He rewrote and enlarged " Darwin among the Machines " and it was republished as " The Mechanical Creation," signed " S.B." in 1865 in *The Reasoner*, a paper edited by G. J. Holyoake. We have it on Butler's later testimony that about this time he wrote the passages that later were incorporated in *Erewhon* on " The World of the Unborn," the Musical Banks, and the trial of a man for being in consumption.

In 1865 he printed a pamphlet, which he had begun to write in New Zealand, entitled *The*

*Evidence for the Resurrection of Jesus Christ as given
by the Four Evangelists critically examined.* In the
preface he wrote:

> My chief regret is that no publisher of
> position will publish heresy so rank as mine.
> . . . It stands just thus. A man has remarks
> to make on certain discrepancies of the four
> Evangelists, remarks which must occur to
> anyone who has tried to put the four narra-
> tives together, and which, even if they be
> erroneous, should be published in order that
> their error may be publicly exposed instead of
> being latently held by hundreds; and yet no
> publisher of position can make them public, even
> if he would, without doing himself a greater
> injury than he would be warranted in doing.

The author's name did not appear, nor did that
of Williams and Norgate, who had it printed for
him. It was a paper covered brochure, $7\frac{1}{2} \times 5$,
of viii + 48 pages. The pamphlet argues that all
the miracles other than the resurrection of Jesus
are insufficiently attested to establish Christianity
on a miraculous basis, and therefore the resurrection is crucial for this purpose: it examines the
evidence and comes to the conclusion that the
most generous interpretation of it is compatible
only with the theory that Jesus did not die but
swooned.

Butler sent a copy to Darwin and a correspondence ensued. In it Darwin wrote to Butler speaking of " your rare powers of writing."

By 1867 Butler had transferred his studentship in art to Heatherley's.

In 1869–70 Butler went abroad for his health, travelling, seeing pictures, for four months. In the spring of 1870 he met a Russian lady. When she was leaving she said, " *Et maintenant, monsieur, vous aller créer.*" " This sank into me and pained me," wrote Butler later. He had been studying other people's work and had been postponing creating. He ought to have started, or rather kept on, creating. He went home resolved to do at any rate something in literature if not in painting.

Broome, a New Zealand friend, was in England about this time, before being appointed Governor of Western Australia, and called on Butler and incidentally suggested that the latter should rewrite his New Zealand articles. So Butler set to work in his spare time. He took for a starting point the letter about " Darwin among the Machines," which he had rewritten as " The Mechanical Creation," and again rewrote it as " The Book of the Machines." He also

rewrote " The World of the Unborn " and turned
the two articles referred to above into " The
Musical Banks " and " An Erewhonian Trial."
These sections, with a few sentences which he
took from memory out of *A First Year in Canterbury Settlement* were all of *Erewhon* that was
written before 1870.

Butler at this time had two friends, a man and
a woman, who had a very stimulating effect
upon him. The most brilliant man that he
thought he had ever known was T. W. G.
Butler. He and Butler were not related,
although they used to fancy they could detect a
family resemblance.   In 1870 or 1871, at Heatherley's, Butler met Miss Eliza Mary Ann Savage,
who was to him uniquely " sympathetic."

Early in 1871 he wrote to her, " I have nearly
finished my book. . . . Will you read the MS. by
small instalments? . . . I am not at all sure that
I shall publish it, and you may save me from
committing a grave indiscretion. . . . I should
very much like your opinion." She accepted,
and Butler henceforward until her death submitted all his MSS. to her and remodelled them
in accordance with her criticisms and suggestions.

In thinking of Butler writing *Erewhon* we may
perhaps remind ourselves that he felt himself
strongly drawn to candour, to speaking the truth

as far as possible, to escaping from the blunders
of convention, of the herd instinct. He was
conscious of things that ordinary people are not
conscious of—he was hurt by things that do
not hurt ordinary people. Like other eminent
writers, he was a keen and penetrating critic of
himself. He was always trying to criticize his
strongest convictions and say to himself, " After
all, you may be wrong, and you must not be guilty
of bad manners." Irony naturally appeals to
the clever who are also sensitive, on the ground
that it enables them to escape wearing their heart
on their sleeve; moreover, the stupid will not
understand; the clever will understand and, if
they are good, will agree; if they are not good,
they will deserve their pain.

Butler's courtesy had the savour of old-world
gallantry. He wrote to Miss Savage, " Can you
name a time and place when and where I can
trespass on your good nature further ? And yet
I cannot call it trespassing, for one can only
trespass on things which have bounds, and your
good nature has none."

In some autobiographical notes written about
1883, Butler said of this time, " I wrote *Erewhon*
with great difficulty. It seemed to me that it
would never get long enough. There were
some things I wanted to say and was sufficiently

clear about, but they all lay in a nutshell." In 1871 *Erewhon* was finished except for the last twenty pages and a sentence or two inserted from time to time here and there in the book, when there appeared an advertisement of a book entitled *The Coming Race*. A friend having called Butler's attention to one of the first of these advertisements and suggested that it probably referred to a work of character similar to his own, he sent the MS. to Chapman & Hall. Their reader, George Meredith, rejected it.

Butler went abroad and eventually came to Varallo-Sesia, where, he had heard, there was a Sacro Monte with frescoed chapels full of remarkable life-size, terra-cotta, painted and clothed figures representing scenes from the life of Christ.

After his return, on December 18 he wrote to Miss Savage, " Trübner & Co. have my book again. They never so much as looked at it before, and said they supposed it had something to do with the Contagious Diseases Act. Now I am to pay their reader a guinea for reading it." In 1872, probably in January, he wrote to Miss Savage, " I write a line to say that I have just had from Trübner & Co. a very favourable report of my MS. I could wish nothing handsomer. Still, Trübner does not say whether he will take

the risk or no. When and where shall I meet you
and show you the letter? I daresay it is all hum-
bug and you will see through it directly, but I
bolted it whole. If Trübner won't take the risk,
I'll get the money from somewhere or other."

In 1872 Shrewsbury School was looking for a
new site and there was a possibility that the
Whitehall fields could be sold for this purpose.
Butler was again, as in 1857, asked to consent to
the sale, but this time he refused. He consulted
a solicitor, who told him that in the sale of 1857
he had been taken advantage of, and advised
proceedings to have it cancelled. Butler wrote
to his father and "a long and angry correspondence ensued." Butler asked that his interest
in the estate be made an absolute instead of a
contingent reversion. This would enable him
to anticipate it, as the property would become
part of his estate on his father's death, whether
he survived his father or not. An absolute
reversion was good security, a contingent one
was not. Butler said plainly that he had been
cheated and suggested this arrangement as
compensation and as the price of joining in the
sale. His relatives refused.

Even Mrs. Garnett, whose book, *Samuel
Butler and his Family Relations*, is a defence of
Butler's family, " cannot acquit Canon Butler

from grave blame." He was "ungenerous" and tyrannical, still he did not mean to be dishonest. It was merely that "he could not grasp Sam's point. . . . It was a blunder and a cruel one."

In the MS. of *Erewhon* was a passage telling of the trial of "a youth barely arrived at man's estate who was charged with having been swindled out of a large property during his minority by his guardian, who was also one of his nearest relations. . . . The lad, who was undefended, pleaded that he was young, inexperienced, greatly in awe of his guardian, and without professional advice. 'Young man,' said the judge sternly, 'do not talk nonsense. People have no right to be young, inexperienced, greatly in awe of their guardians, and without independent professional advice.'"

Butler had to publish the book at his own risk and—owing to his generosity to Pauli—he had no money to do it with. In 1901 he wrote, "Henry Hoare lent me the money, otherwise I do not know what I should have done."

Of the MS. of *Erewhon* Butler wrote to Miss Savage while he was correcting proof, "It reads very well . . . even Pauli, who had been the most freezing critic hitherto, (in so far as he could be got to listen to a passage here and there) thawed a little as he read; the fact is, he is frightened

out of his wits about it, and expects my father to
cut me off with a shilling; but he dares not say
this because he knows I should fly at him if he
advised me to let my father's will enter into the
matter at all." Nevertheless, the passage about
the young man swindled by one of his nearest
relations was omitted. (It appeared for the first
time in the revised edition of 1901.)[1]

The novel, *The Coming Race*, had been published
in 1871. Butler was told that its heroine was
called " Zee." Now one of the characters in
Erewhon was a lady called " Zelora." Butler
altered her name to " Zulora." *The Coming
Race* Butler did not see, nor even a review of it,
until he sent back the last revises of *Erewhon* to
the printer. He was surprised at the many little
points of similarity between the two books in
spite of their entire independence of each other.

Butler, of course, was a very eager nature: he
had to rope himself in and exercise great restraint.
In 1872 he wrote to Miss Savage, " I know you
are ill. I knew you were ill yesterday, and yet I
plagued you with my book. I thought at times
how selfish I was—nevertheless I did it. . . . I
strongly suspect that your people plague you—
very strongly; it is a wicked world, and there

[1] For the last four paragraphs, Stillman, *Samuel Butler*, pp. 103,
104, 107, 108.

are few who fail to make themselves unpleasant if they have the power to do so."

Erewhon was published in 1872. It was anonymous. The first copy Butler gave to Miss Savage with an inscription.

"EREWHON"

The mottos on the title-pages of Butler's books are very significant. That for *Erewhon* is a sentence from Aristotle paraphrased thus— "There is no action save upon a balance of considerations." This symbolizes the fact that Butler had arrived at the philosophical doctrine of relativity, and indeed he did thoroughly carry it out, in particular in ethics.

Butler hit upon the idea of giving descriptions of New Zealand as if the author had found his way into a hitherto undiscovered country, thus creating verisimilitude. Once there he could express things that had exercised him—that conventions and conventional people were often the opposite of what they pretended to be; that evolution led to revolution in thought. He neither had solved, nor did he pretend to have solved, the problems, but in the book he repeated what he had already written about his pamphlet on the Resurrection, "People ought to say openly what they think and why they think it. After all, they may be mistaken, and, if so, it is for their

own and the general welfare that they should let
their error be seen as distinctly as possible so
that it may be more easily refuted."

Erewhon (" nowhere ") is England with things
that it has and ought not to have and also with
things it hasn't and ought to have. Butler put
forward the idea of crime being treated as
disease. He pointed out that totally inadequate
provision is made for the care of the moral
character of the people at large. In general he
went in for religious, social, moral, artistic and
educational satire. Special attention is given to
the Colleges of Unreason, run by people who
were cursed with the fear of giving themselves
away. Special attention is also given to the
problem of Mechanism. Butler perceived early
the peril of the machine and uttered the warning.

Butler's humour and subtlety led him to
represent the author as a philistine. His social
criticism—for example, of women—is " modern."
" I fancy she had resolved to marry me although
I had never so much as hinted at her doing so."
Butler, like other writers of insight, had only to
speak the truth to be considered as having uttered
paradox—e.g., " Ill luck of any kind, or even ill
treatment at the hands of others, is considered
an offence against society, inasmuch as it makes
people uncomfortable to hear of it. Loss of

fortune, therefore, or loss of some dear friend on whom another was much dependent, is punished hardly less severely than moral delinquency."

Medical men of course come in for exposure. Butler argued for moral delinquencies being treated, however, in the same scientific spirit as physical diseases are dealt with. Children should be told what they are in for and how to guard against dangers in adult life. Ministers of religion should really know about the sins they are supposed to deal with in other people. Butler was sceptical of the virtue of the Victorian. " Be not righteous overmuch," he quoted, and he satirized the " unco guid." His verisimilitude is close: he introduced things from real life with only the barely necessary alterations.

Butler was deeply impressed by the fact that overt crime was largely due to causes beyond the control of the criminal, and yet the criminal had against him the huge convention that he could have controlled himself adequately. Property, marriage, the law are largely organized theft, lust and revenge; they are backed by the tremendous force of instinct-feeling. The overwhelming power of convention, of the herd instinct, impressed Butler deeply—to see a judge, for example, so noble in many ways, and yet unable to emanci-

pate himself from convention. Butler had deep
sympathy with people who suffered—for
example, those who suffered from the crudity of
our methods of dealing with " criminals." We
all know of the existence of such evils, " yet
people were too indolent, and too indifferent to
suffering not their own to bestir themselves to
putting an end to them." But it was decided to
fine one lot and imprison another. " The mass
of the people were well pleased with the existing
arrangements, and believe that treatment of
criminals leaves little or nothing to be desired."
Butler's positive solution of the problem was
internment.

One of the things in *Erewhon* that are not in
England but ought to be is the love of beauty.
Statues are put up chronicling some unusual
excellence of beauty of form. Among the
people, beauty of manners is predominant. On
the other hand, in the Erewhonians Butler
satirized the unmusical in our midst.

He satirized people who speak about art
without really understanding it. He attacked
the existing practice in erecting statues. " They
were generally foisted on the public by some
coterie that was trying to exalt itself in exalting
someone else, and not infrequently they had no
other inception than the desire on the part of

some member of the coterie to find a job for a young sculptor to whom his daughter was engaged." Hence people have to live with the image, often enough, of " some wordy windbag whose cowardice had cost the country untold loss in blood and money." (It would be too perilous to speculate as to whom Butler was thinking of.) Artistically most of the statues are dead, putrefying: there is no artistic sanitation —no drainage, so to speak, whereby they might be carried out of the system. Perhaps a simpler plan, says Butler, would have been to forbid the erection of a statue to any public man or woman until he or she had been dead at least one hundred years, and even then to insist on reconsideration of the claims of the deceased and the merit of the statue every fifty years.

An art, says Butler, can be learnt only in the workshop of those who are earning their bread by it. There is no way of making an aged art young again; it is better for it to be dead than dying. All the noblest arts hold in perfection for a very little moment. They soon reach a height from which they begin to decline. Academies of art pretend to sell the holy spirit; pupils come in the hope of selling it later on; and are struck purblind as a punishment.

Butler satirized the churches as Musical Banks

which dealt in a double currency—that which was valid in the world and that which was valid only in the pretence of the banks.[1] He observed that the attitude of most church-goers had "a certain air of reserve"; they did not vigorously believe in religion; most wished simply to be considered "respectable." "They carried their purses in their hands not exactly ostentatiously, yet just so that those who met them should see whither they were going." Most were ladies. "There was a something of regret, a something as though they would like to take me with them, but did not like to ask me, and yet as though I were hardly to ask to be taken." After "a little parleying and many inquiries as to whether I was perfectly sure that I myself wished to go," he was allowed to go.

In his description of an ancient cathedral Butler writes fine prose:

> On either side there were beautiful trees wherein the birds were busy by the hundred, and a number of quaint but substantial houses of singularly comfortable appearance; they were situated in the midst of orchards and gardens, and gave me an impression of great peace and plenty.

[1] It is perhaps worth noting that this situation existed literally among the Jews of Palestine at the time of Christ.

D

Indeed it had been no error to say that this building was one that appealed to the imagination; it did more—it carried both imagination and judgment by storm. It was an epic in stone and marble, and so powerful was the effect it produced on me that as I beheld it I was charmed and melted. I felt more conscious of the existence of a remote past. One knows of this always, but the knowledge is never so living as in the actual presence of some witness to the life of bygone ages. I felt how short a space of human life was the period of our own existence. I was more impressed by my own littleness, and much more inclinable to believe that the people whose sense of the fitness of things was equal to the upraising of so serene a handiwork were hardly likely to be wrong in the conclusions they might come to on any subject.

But the music the narrator found in the cathedral!—" The singers seemed to have derived their inspiration from the songs of birds and the wailing of the wind, which last they tried to imitate in melancholy cadences that at times degenerated into a howl. To my thinking the noise was hideous, but it produced a wonderful effect upon my companions, who professed themselves much moved."

He was struck by the building being so nearly empty and the comparative number of clergy. Although the spiritual coinage was professed to be much more valuable than the natural, when Higgs tried to tip a verger with it, he was so angry that Higgs had to pacify him with a piece of the other kind of money. The clergy read as one who, putting his hand into an antique coffer, pulled out a quantity of metal pieces apparently at random and handed them over without counting them. Payments were made in the other coinage; the spiritual money was not used except in church.

Religion in the churches did not demonstrate its value. " In commercial panics, and in times of general distress, the people as a mass did not so much as think of turning to these banks. A few might do so, some from habit and early training, some from the instinct that prompts us to catch at any straw when we think ourselves drowning, but few from a genuine belief that the Musical Banks could save them " from spiritual ruin.

But the churches were unwilling to change. A clergyman said " that it had been more or less true till lately; but that now they had put fresh stained glass windows . . . the presidents, moreover, had taken to riding in omnibuses and talking nicely to people. . . . ' But haven't you done

anything to the money itself?' said I, timidly.
'It is not necessary,' he rejoined; 'not in the
least necessary, I assure you.'"

The faces of the clergymen "did not please
me; they lacked, with few exceptions, the true
Erewhonian frankness; and an equal number
from any other class would have looked happier
and better men. When I met them in the streets,
they did not seem like other people, but had, as a
general rule, a cramped expression upon their
faces which pained and depressed me." " In
nine cases out of ten they were well-meaning
persons; they were in the main very poorly
paid; their [characters] were as a rule above
suspicion; but they had had the misfortune to
have been betrayed into a false position at an age
when their judgment was not mature, and after
having been kept in studied ignorance of the real
difficulties of the system."

" So far as I could see, fully ninety per cent.
of the population of the metropolis looked upon
these banks with something not far removed from
contempt."

On the subject of education Butler naturally
had something to say. As, since his time,
education has been carried back to pre-natal
conditions, so Butler dealt with pre-natal considerations. He reacted against the idea that a

being should be sentenced to "undergo the chances and changes of this mortal life without any option in the matter." Once born, the Erewhonians were brought up to worship " good form." Butler's main doctrine in education was that " such things as kindly training, a good example and an enlightened regard to one's own welfare " were able to keep a man straight.

Butler was not in favour of the place given to the classics and mathematics in the educational system of his time. It seemed to him wrong to give so much time to "barren exercises " such as Greek and Latin "verses " when "our own civilization presented problems by the hundred which cried aloud for solution and would have paid the solver handsomely." There is an education of the wrong kind, moreover, that goes on in and through the official education—of Inconsistency and Evasion: "there is hardly any inconsistency so glaring but they soon learn to defend it, or injunction so clear that they cannot find some pretext for disregarding it."

To the economic factor in life he attached first importance and was in favour of the frank recognition of its importance. " He who makes a colossal fortune in the hosiery trade, and by his energy has succeeded in reducing the price of woollen goods by the thousandth part of a penny in the pound—this man is worth ten professional philanthropists." How " often does it happen that we perceive a man to have all sorts of good qualities except money, and feel that his real duty lies in getting every halfpenny that he can persuade others to pay him for his services, and becoming rich."[1]

If you ask the author of *Erewhon* what means we are to take to bring about reforms, he has one piece of advice to give—the appeal to economy— " appealing to men's pockets, in which they have generally something of their own " rather " than to their heads, which contain for the most part little but borrowed or stolen property."

Below all the irony of *Erewhon* is a really deep feeling and a really deep philosophy. Even in metaphysics Butler has his word to say, as, for example, this doctrine of time, which has something in it of anticipation of recent scientific philosophy:

The future is there as much as the past, only we may not see it. Is it not in the past, and must not the past alter before the future can do so ? The future depends on the present, and the present (whose existence is only one of

[1] This is the doctrine taken up and referred to by Mr. Bernard Shaw in the preface to *Major Barbara*.

these minor compromises of which human life is full—for it lives only on sufferance of the past and future) depends on the past.

The ultimate philosophical faith that Butler had arrived at was that the ultimate values in life are spiritual. Most people, he held, have never been born into them.

Butler wrote at this time, " I think I've about said all that I have to say." Later he wrote, " If I had had another page of matter in me, it would have gone into *Erewhon*." All he had in mind to write and publish was a volume of essays, all serious and therefore, he wrote, they would not be read.

Erewhon was assumed in some circles to be the work of the author of *The Coming Race* (who was, of course, Lord Lytton); at least it was thought that *Erewhon* had been expressly modelled on *The Coming Race*.

It is of interest and some importance to know how *Erewhon* was received, and I therefore transcribe (but in chronological order) some of the excerpts from reviews printed in a later edition, all of which appeared in 1872:

Echo, April 9: " A very clever, striking and original book."

Pall Mall Gazette, April 12: " A very

remarkable book...it is obvious that a change is coming over the whole scope of our laws; and anyone who will take the trouble to read, mark, learn and inwardly digest the little book of which we have spoken, and will do all this in a philosophical spirit, will probably come to the conclusion that it is as reasonable, and as desirable for the good of society, to send to prison the man who *will* take typhus fever, as to send to hospital the woman who couldn't be restrained from murder."

Spectator, April 20: "It is obvious that we have amongst us a satirist of very remarkable literary power, as well as of a very cynical turn of mind. Since the days of Swift nothing has been written abler in its peculiar way, and certainly nothing more thoroughly bitter and contemptuous in its drift, than the little book called *Erewhon or Over the Range*."

Examiner, April 27: "It deserves careful reading; and will probably find its way where a more sermon-like book would only repel. It shakes the dry bones of our moral and religious formulae to some good purpose, let us hope. Not a few who will be drawn to the book for amusement only will find concealed under the mask of comedy not a little wholesome truth and wisdom."

Vanity Fair, May 4: " *Erewhon* has attracted a great deal of notice. The writer has by some reviewers been compared with Swift, by others he is decried with an animus that seems equally to bear witness to satirical merit."

Scotsman, May 17: " Since Swift wrote *Gulliver's Travels* and the *Tale of a Tub* he has had many imitators and no equals; but there will be general agreement that *Erewhon* should take a prominent place after Swift. There are passages in it of great power, and the satire is throughout pungent. . . . There is not a page that has not point, sparkle, humour and satire."

Illustrated London News, May 18: " This part of the book is as interesting as *Robinson Crusoe*; the remaining parts have more affinity to *Gulliver's Travels*."

Other reviews quoted are of a usual patronizing kind.

Butler wrote to Darwin to explain that in the chapter on machines he was not tilting at him but rather at the methods of Butler of the *Analogy*, meaning, " See how easy it is to be plausible, and what absurd propositions can be defended by a little ingenuity." Soon after, Butler was invited to Darwin's and paid two visits. He thus got to know the family and for some years he was intimate with Francis.

The authorship of *Erewhon* was fairly well
known. In *The Athenaeum* for May 25 the following appeared in " Literary Gossip ": " It is said
that *Erewhon*, the allegorical romance which we
reviewed some little time ago, is the production
of Mr. Butler, who was for some years a settler
in New Zealand, and who is tolerably well-
known in London artistic circles." The *Drawing
Room Gazette*, with which Miss Savage was
connected, also revealed Butler's authorship of
Erewhon on the same day. Butler is described as
" a gentleman well known in London society,
and an artist of some reputation and great pro-
mise." Immediately after it was thus made
known that the author of *Erewhon* was an unknown
the weekly sale fell from fifty to two or three.

The *Drawing Room Gazette* for June 8 had the
following in a notice of *Erewhon*: " In fact, he
[the hero] is a prig, and never has the character
been more amusingly set forth. Molière would
not have disowned it, and, indeed, there are
touches here and there which, if it were possible
for departed spirits to be moved by earthly passions, would make him writhe with envy. . . .
It is enough to say that the lash of the author's
satire falls fiercely on many of our social and
religious hypocrisies and unrealities." In a
notice in the German *Grenzboten* appeared the

following: " ' Erewhon oder Jenseits der Berge,' so würde ich auf deutsch ein Buch nennen, welches soeben in London bei Trübner u. Comp. erschienen ist, und das wir in einigen von seinen Capiteln dem Besten, was die englische Humoristik Swiftschen Stiles geleistet hat, an die Seite stellen möchten."

The first edition of *Erewhon* was of 750 to 1,000 copies. A second edition was called for and was published, in cheaper form than the first, in 1872. Butler wrote a new preface beginning, " Having been enabled by the kindness of the public to get through an unusually large edition in a very short time. . . . " He expressed regret that in the chapter on machines he should have been thought to be satirizing Darwin, for whom he had the most profound admiration. He adds that the Erewhonians " really were a very difficult people to understand. The most glaring anomalies seemed to afford them no intellectual inconvenience ; neither, provided that they did not actually see the money dropping out of their pockets nor suffer immediate physical pain, would they listen to any arguments as to the waste of money and happiness which their folly cost them."

Butler " knew his own weight." He wrote to Miss Savage that to his father " I bounced about the success of my book through mistaken policy, and said I believed I had it in my power to put my name in the front rank among writers of my time and country—an unwise and boastful thing to say, and I had better not have said it."

The impression made by *Erewhon* led to Butler's having to undergo a period of lionizing in a small way. He was not the sort of man to be a success in this. " A certain diffidence never left him." He looked upon himself as a painter and upon *Erewhon* as an interruption.

(A third edition was issued in 1872; a fourth and fifth edition, with the author's name, in 1873; and there were at least four more reprints or reissues before 1901, when it was enlarged by 60 pages to prolong copyright. It was published in Dutch in 1873; in German in 1879; in French in 1920; and in Spanish.)

Butler at the time of the publication of *Erewhon*, in 1872, wrote one or two musical critiques for *The Drawing Room Gazette*.

About this time he decided to call in his money invested in New Zealand—for Pauli's sake. His mortgagee was his friend Moorhouse, and the feeling that the calling in of the mortgage

might have injured the latter hurt Butler to the
end of his life, although the feeling was in fact
baseless.

"THE FAIR HAVEN"

We have seen that Butler felt that he had nothing
more to write. Nevertheless, within a few weeks,
he remembered his pamphlet on the Resurrection
and thought he might make a book of it. He
could publish it anonymously—nay, pseudony-
mously: he would write the book as if it had
been written by an imagined individual: he
might, pursuing this line, make some response to
appeals to write a novel: he would use ironic
humour, for a serious book, published as such,
would not be read. So he thought he would
write one more book. He set to work, sub-
mitting it to Miss Savage.

Butler at this time wrote a remarkable piece of
self-criticism:

Fearless himself, he could not understand
the fears felt by others; and this was perhaps
his greatest sympathetic weakness. . . . The
force of early bias and education, the force
of intellectual surroundings, the force of natural
timidity, the force of dulness, were things which
he could make allowance for in any other
age and among any other people than his own;

but as belonging to England and the Nineteenth Century they had no place in his theory
of Nature; they were inconceivable, unnatural,
unpardonable. The subtlety of his mind was
a more serious source of danger to him, though
I do not know that he greatly lost by it in
comparison with what he gained: his sense,
however, of distinctions was so fine that it
would sometimes distract his attention from
points of infinitely greater importance in
connexion with his subject than the particular
distinction he was trying to establish at the
moment.

He could not understand why one may not say
what one honestly believes.

Here are some of the convictions that Butler
had arrived at:

O what suicidal folly there is even in the
remotest semblance of unfairness.

Persons make great reputations by telling the
people what they like to hear, what they
perfectly well know, and are in no particular
danger of forgetting.

It is one thing to see no merit in a picture,
and another to see no merit in a picture when
one is told it is by Raphael. We are few of us
able to stand up against the prestige of a great
name: our self-love is alarmed lest we should

be deficient in taste, or, worst still, lest we should be considered to be so; as if it could matter to any right-minded person whether the world considered him to be of good taste or not, in comparison with the keeping of his own soul truthful with itself.

The man who lets himself be bored is even more contemptible than the bore. He who puts up with shoddy pictures, shoddy music, shoddy morality, shoddy society, is more despicable than he who is the prime agent in any of these things.

O if men would but leave off lying to themselves! If they would but learn the sacredness of their own likes and dislikes, and exercise their moral discrimination, making clear to themselves what it is that they really love and venerate! There is no such enemy to mankind as moral cowardice. A downright vulgar, self-interested and unblushing liar is a higher being than the moral cur whose likes and dislikes are at the beck and call of bullies that stand between himself and his own soul. Such a creature gives up the most sacred of all his rights for something more unsubstantial than a mess of pottage—a mental serf too abject to know even that he is being wronged. Wretched emasculator of his own reason, whose jejune timidity and want of vitality are thus omnipresent in the most sacred chambers of his heart !

We can forgive a man for almost any false-hood, provided we feel that he was under strong temptation and well knew that he was deceiving. He has done wrong—still we can understand it, and he may yet have some useful stuff about him—but what can we feel towards one who for a small motive tells lies even to himself, and does not know that he is lying? What useless figwood lumber must not such a thing be made of, and what lies will there not come out of it, falling in every direction upon all who come within its reach? The common self-deceiver of modern society is a more dangerous and contemptible object than almost any ordinary felon, a matter upon which those who do not deceive themselves need no enlightenment.

There is no policy so unwise as fear in a good cause: the bold course is also the wise one.

Of all those engaged in training our young men for Holy Orders, of all our Bishops and tutors at colleges, whose very profession it is to be lovers of truth and candour, who are paid for being so, and who are mere shams and wolves in sheep's clothing if they are not ever

on the look-out for falsehood, to make war
upon it as the enemy of our souls—not one,
no, not a single one, so far as I know, has raised
his voice in protest. If a man has not lost
his power of weeping, let him weep for this;
if there is any who realizes the crime of self-
deception, as perhaps the most subtle and
hideous of all forms of sin, let him lift up his
voice and proclaim it now, for the times are
not of peace, but of a sowing of wind for the
reaping of whirlwinds, and of the calm that is
in the centre of the hurricane.

These were Butler's views, slightly coloured in
the form of expression for the purposes of the
book. It might appear that for a man of these
opinions, irony would be impossible. But it
cannot be denied that to clever people it is a
temptation to enjoy their superiority and find
humour in misunderstanding by the stupid.
Again, there are things that a man thinks ought
to be said, although he is not prepared to back
them with his full personal responsibility. A
dramatist, like Mr. Shaw, can use his characters
for this purpose. Butler used his fictions similarly. The orthodox had treated Butler badly:
he believed their position to be largely pernicious.
He was David against Goliath: he would fight
them: he was a bonnie fighter. There is no

doubt that Butler wanted to be taken notice of: he would let them see that he mattered.

Let him write a straightforward treatise on the Resurrection, as he had done, and nobody would read it. How could he get the orthodox to read his arguments? By pretending to *answer* objections to the Resurrection, by pretending to be a pathetically earnest Christian and thus, pretending to meet objections, introducing objections. He wrote that we " must consider rather what we can get them to take than what we should like to give them: ' Be ye wise as serpents and harmless as doves.' " In *Erewhon* Butler had pretended to be a philistine. In *The Fair Haven* he pretended to be an Evangelical Churchman, but, as in *Erewhon*, was saying both what ought to be and was not, and what ought not to be and was.

As Butler himself feared, his sense of the importance of certain things was not that of any but a very few. Hence the book is largely taken up with arguments that to most people do not seem worth while, however able and true they are.

If Butler was attacking historical Christianity, as he was, what had he to put in its place? Well, first of all, he objected to an ideal that did not admit of improvement. He preferred catholicity

in the ideal. The absolute cannot be expressed
fully in the concrete. Hence that is best which
symbolically suggests what is unexpressed, which
does not pretend to be perfect but frankly
acknowledges imperfection. As against the
asceticism of Christianity the forms of ancient
Greek art are to be preferred.

Butler objected to religion offering empty
consolations: this was the false coinage of the
Erewhonian banks.

To the artisan, for instance, who may have
long been out of work, or who may have
suffered from the greed and selfishness of his
employers, or again, to the farm labourer who
has been discharged perhaps at the approach
of winter, the parable of "the Labourers in
the Vineyard" offers itself as a divinely
sanctioned picture of the dealings of God with
man; few but those who have mixed with the
less educated classes can have an idea of the
priceless comfort which this parable affords
daily to those whose lot it has been to remain
unemployed when their more fortunate
brethren have been in full work.

Here Butler's irony is of course grim, but there
is also in it another, and a more subtle, irony: he
saw at the same time that many *were* comforted
by such teaching. "Hope is given by these

sayings to many whose lives would be otherwise very nearly hopeless."

He criticized the parables of the Prodigal Son and of the Unjust Steward, and the doctrine of Providence. (When Mr. Desmond MacCarthy told Butler that he was going in for literature as his profession, Butler said, "Doubtless the Lord will provide your daily bread, although possibly not with the regularity of the professional baker.")

Here is another example of Butler's irony in *The Fair Haven*: "those who deny the Death and Resurrection of our Lord call upon us to believe that an immense multitude of most truthful and amiable people are no less deceivers of their own selves and others than Mohammedans, Jews and Buddhists are."

Butler, as we have seen, decided to support the mystification of the authorship of *The Fair Haven* with a memoir of the supposed author. This gave him further opportunity to comply with requests for a "novel" and to express his deep-seated regrets in respect of his own experience, in the hope that the evil that was and ought not to be might be done away and the way made smoother for others. It gave him, again, a further and subtle opportunity for irony.

The father in the biography is the opposite of Butler's father:

> a singularly gentle and humorous playmate who doted on us both and never spoke unkindly. Whenever we pleased him, no matter how little, he never failed to thank us.

> He did indeed well know the art of becoming idolized by his children, and dearly did he prize the results of his own proficiency; yet truly there was no art about it; it all arose spontaneously from the well-spring of a sympathetic nature which knew how to feel as others felt.

In reality Butler's experience was that " as love casteth out fear, so fear love." The mother in the pseudo-biography is said by Festing Jones to be an exact portrait of Butler's mother, but I hazard the opinion that it is a portrait of Butler's father.

Butler reproduces his discovery that persons and things were not as they appeared to be—that women were not solid from the waist down; that animals, from the point of view of food, were hollow. He had a hankering after neatness, truth, exactitude. It took him a long time to discover the relativity of things—" what thick and sticky fluids were air and water ;" that speech, instead of being a perfect messenger of thought, was nothing but a shuffler and a loiterer; that the half can be greater than the whole. He came to some conclusions about permanent truth:

All permanent truth is as one of those coal measures, a seam of which lies near the surface, and even crops up above the ground, but which is generally of an inferior quality and soon worked out; beneath it there comes a layer of sand and clay, and then at last the true seam of precious quality and in virtually inexhaustible supply. The truth which is on the surface is rarely the whole truth. It is seldom until this has been worked out and done with—as in the case of the apparent flatness of the earth—that unchangeable truth is discovered.

It is indeed incongruous to have to record side by side with Butler's preoccupation with religion that from 1872 he had a mistress, a Frenchwoman living in London, to whom alone, thereafter until her death, he went. Butler's attitude to prostitution I have discussed above. His sexual life was merely physical. This woman was twenty-one—Butler was thirty-seven—when he picked her up in Islington one evening. She was " a simple, honest, and shrewd woman who

was not in the least ashamed of her profession, a
prostitute of good character, kind heart and
amiability who brought to her career the thrifty
and respectable virtues of the *petite bourgeoisie*
from which she sprang. A devout Catholic,
she fed her cat with hot cross buns on a Friday
and even tried (unsuccessfully) to make Butler
faire maigre."[1]   Perhaps some light is afforded on
such a woman by a passage in Unamuno's *The
Life of Don Quixote and Sancho*: "The kindly
Maritornes loved greatly, in her own way, and
should be pardoned for her affairs with carriers
since she indulged them out of pure softness of
heart. You may well believe that the beautiful
Asturian wench sought rather to give than to
receive pleasure; if she yielded her person, it was,
as happens to not a few Maritornes, in order not
to see men fret and suffer. She wished to purify
the carriers of the base desires that soiled their
minds, and to leave them clean for their work."[2]
This does not, of course, settle her innocence or
Butler's. I can only repeat that, in view of
Butler's development otherwise, it is to me staggering that he did not achieve a more honourable
solution of his problem.

Whether it was original or not, this woman

[1] Mrs. Stillman, *Samuel Butler*, p. 169.
[2] Quoted by Bullett, *The Testament of Light*, No. 12.

uttered one of the best comments that have yet been made on Butler—" Il sait tout, il ne sait rien, il est poète."

Writing to Miss Savage in March, 1873, shortly before the publication of *The Fair Haven*, Butler said, " I should hope that attacks on *The Fair Haven* will give me an opportunity of excusing myself, and if so I shall endeavour that the excuse may be worse than the fault it is intended to excuse. . . . I daresay I shall get into a row—at least I hope I shall."

The book was published with the title, " The Fair Haven, A work in defence of the miraculous element in our Lord's ministry upon earth, both as against Rationalistic impugners and certain Orthodox defenders, by the late John Pickard Owen, Edited by William Bickersteth Owen, with a Memoir of the Author." It was published by Trübner at Butler's risk.

I confess that it seems to me that Butler was somewhat unscrupulous, carrying a practical joke too far, making the end justify the means.

He wrote to Fleay (the Shakespeare scholar, who was a friend) immediately after publication that if the book fell flat, he would at once connect it with *Erewhon* and advertise it as by the same author. He was afraid, he said, that the book was

dull: here his acute self-criticism comes out
again, for to a considerable extent it is.

He sent a copy to Darwin, who, in reply, wrote,
"You will soon be universally known. . . .
What has struck me so much in your book is
your dramatic power—that is to say, the way in
which you earnestly and thoroughly assume the
character and think the thoughts of the man you
pretend to be.   Hence I conclude that you could
write a really good novel."

Butler's mother, while holidaying in the south
of France, became gravely ill. His business
quarrel with his father was dropped for the time.
Butler wrote to Miss Savage, "What pains me
is that I cannot begin to regain the affection now
which, alas! I have long since ceased to feel."
At the beginning of April he went to his mother.
She died a few days after his arrival.   Butler's
father gave him to understand that her death
was caused by his having published *Erewhon*.

Some reviewers and divines, even of high
standing, greeted *The Fair Haven* solemnly as a
defence of orthodoxy.   Canon Ainger sent it to
a friend whom he wished to convert.   A theological paper, *The Rock*, felt obliged to devote two
reviews to it and walked right into Butler's trap.

So did *The Scotsman*. Other reviewers either " smelt a rat " or exposed the pretence.

The book sold poorly, and in the autumn of 1873 Butler carried out his intention and had a re-issue as a " second edition " with a new title-page revealing the authorship, and a new additional preface, dealing with the book frankly, but also side by side with the frankness, ironically.

Butler's prospects of becoming a successful author were—there can be little doubt—adversely affected by *The Fair Haven* through the distrust it evoked. He had, however, come to feel that there were one or two further books that he must write, and now he set to work on a novel. He did not want " purpose " in it, but he had things he wanted to say in criticism of things that had come home to him in his own experience.

At this time he had sold a few pictures from the Academy. He was painting Mr. Heatherley in his studio mending a skeleton —" background, all the pots and pans and knicknacks . . . with the Discobolus and half the Ilyssus."

At this time, too, he became implicated, on the strength of the recommendations of his friend Hoare, who was connected with Hoare's Bank, and Pauli and another barrister friend, in an investment in Canada that turned out wrong.

The idea was the extraction of tanning for leather from bark: it was sound, except that the resulting colour was such that the product did not sell. In March, 1874, Hoare failed, and Butler found himself with most of his money gone and with Pauli to support. Throughout this time of trial for Butler, as in many other matters, Miss Savage helped him with most uncommon sense, and she gave him more than that—she gave him sympathy and admiration. Having written to her expressing regret for having written harshly about Hoare, he received the following: " My dear Mr. Butler, I don't think there is anybody quite so good as you are. When I know someone who is, I will tell you."

Butler had been made a director of the Canada company. Some hope of saving part of the money in it was still possible, and he was deputed by his co-directors to go to Canada. Before leaving, he had the pleasure of seeing " Mr. Heatherley's Holiday " in the Royal Academy exhibition, hanging on the line. It attracted a good deal of notice and is now in the Tate Gallery.

From midsummer 1874 Butler did little writing for over a year. He had, however, begun to think about the matters that matured in *Life and Habit*. He wrote some of it after he arrived in

Canada, the purple passage about " the sound of
bells wafted to a high mountain " being written
on Montreal Mountain.

He returned to this country in July for a few
days' conference only. Reporting to Miss
Savage on his writing, within these few days,
he wrote, " No, I will not be didactic—at least I
will watch and pray that I may not be so; but being
didactic is a sin which doth so easily beset me."

The time of investigating the Canadian business
was one of great anxiety for Butler—was he to be
penniless or all right? On returning to Canada,
he remained there for some months, " fighting
fraud of every kind to the best of my ability."
In spite of his own financial peril, he bought back
the shares of those friends whom he had induced
to invest in the company, and contrived that they
did not lose through following his advice.

Miss Savage wrote to him with the encourage-
ment that, in spite of his money difficulties, he
was a very lucky man: " You have great and
varied talents, genius I should say, and you have
so much capacity for so many kinds of enjoy-
ment. You were born with a sweet temper, an
unselfish disposition, and a natural disposition
to deal righteously with your fellow creatures
and power of mind enough to cultivate the
inclination; and yet you want to be rich. I call

you a most unreasonable man. Let the poor,
stupid, disagreeable people have the money (I
think they very often do)—they want it, poor
things!"

We find that, at this time, among the books
Butler read was a translation of *Wilhelm Meister*.
It is characteristic of Butler's courage to be
contra mundum that he wrote to Miss Savage about
it, "Is it good? To me it seems perhaps the
very worst book I have ever read . . . I cannot
remember a single good page or idea. . . . Is it
all a practical joke? If it really is Goethe's *Wilhelm
Meister* that I have been reading I am glad I have
never taken the trouble to learn German. What a
wretch Carlyle must be to run Goethe as he has
done." Butler did not know that Carlyle had
described *Wilhelm Meister* as "bushels of straw
and feathers," although he had added "with here
and there a diamond of the purest water."

Butler did not like Montreal. He wrote, "A
man, a true Montrealler, told me he had a yearning
to get away from civilization: I said we were all
of us given to discontent and seldom knew when
we had got what we wanted. He did not see it,
and I did not mean that he should; but I felt
better for having said it." It was of this time,
too, of course, that he wrote "A Psalm of
Montreal." (He wrote it in 1875.) The humour

in this ought not to obscure the fact that it is a
manifesto of a real religious revolution, an express
protest that beauty is an experience of the divine.

Butler's business affairs in Canada did not
prosper, in spite of all his efforts. He was
involved in litigation. His opponents tried to
get his evidence set aside on the ground that he
was an atheist. He fought them with all his
great resources of ability and courage. As he
wrote to Miss Savage, he hoped it might be truly
said that, if he had fallen among thieves, the
thieves had also fallen among him. As a result
of his efforts, he had reduced the expenses by
£1,600 a year. In the end Butler had left to him,
as his total capital, £2,000.

In spite of this, he went on paying Pauli £200
a year—although for long enough Pauli had
refused to let him have his address. Hitherto
Butler had had £800 a year and had never wanted
more than £300 for his own expenses. His
generosity to Pauli was purely disinterested.

With regard to new sources of income, Butler
still believed that if he honourably did his best,
his work must sell. He never had more than a
few pounds now and then by selling a picture.
For the next twelve years he was in an extremely
embarrassing financial position. He summed up
his Canadian adventure as follows: " I have had

to pay for my experience, but I have got a good
article which will last me my life-time."

To add to his worries, he inferred from something Miss Savage wrote to him that she wanted
to marry him, and he did not want to marry her.
It is doubtful—I discussed this with the late Mr.
Bartholomew and he agreed—whether Miss
Savage meant this at all. But the fact that he
believed she did created of course an extremely
difficult position. Festing Jones in his biography described what happened with admirable
tact: " When this situation arises between a
man and a woman, intercourse cannot be continued for long unless one or the other yields.
Miss Savage yielded," and Butler to the end of his
days felt that she had heaped coals of fire upon
his head—he felt shame and disgrace that she
had treated him nobly whereas he had not
treated her nobly. He wrote, " I never was
placed in a much more difficult position. To
write was to encourage false hopes; not to write
was to be grossly unkind."

Early in life Butler acquired the habit of
carrying a notebook and of writing in it anything
he wanted to remember: it might be something
he had heard someone say; more often it was
something he had heard himself say. In the

autumn of 1874, while he was in Montreal, he
began to keep the series of notebooks which
after his death became famous.

At the end of 1875 Butler returned to England. He began to put together notes he had
been writing on the importance of habit in the
history of life.

In 1876 Butler met Festing Jones, afterwards
his most *fidus Achates*. Music was an initial
and later a strong bond.

Working on the importance of habit in the
history of life, Butler at first treated the ideas he
arrived at as ingenious paradoxes, but presently
he felt that he had made a real discovery. Suppose our organs are machines: how did we come
to have them? On February 18 he wrote a most
remarkable letter to his friend, T. W. G. Butler,
putting the gist of what was going to be *Life and
Habit*; just then he thought he was writing a
pamphlet of twenty-five to thirty pages, but he saw
presently that it would have to be longer than that.

In 1876 he wrote " The Righteous Man,"
surely one of the most powerful things of its
kind ever written:

" THE RIGHTEOUS MAN "

The righteous man will rob none but the
defenceless,

Whatsoever can reckon with him he will
   neither plunder nor kill;
He will steal an egg from a hen or a lamb from
   a ewe,
For his sheep and his hens cannot reckon with
   him hereafter—
They live not in any odour of defencefulness:
Therefore right is with the righteous man, and
   he taketh advantage righteously,
Praising God and plundering.

The righteous man will enslave his horse and
   his dog,
Making them serve for their bare keep and for
   nothing further,
Shooting them, selling them for vivisection
   when they can no longer profit him,
Backbiting them and beating them if they fail
   to please him;
For his horse and his dog can bring no action
   for damages,
Wherefore, then, should he not enslave them,
   shoot them, sell them for vivisection?

But the righteous man will not plunder the
   defenceful—
Not if he be alone and unarmed—for his conscience will smite him:

F

He will not rob a she-bear of her cubs, nor an
    eagle of her eaglets—
Unless he have a rifle to purge him from the
    fear of sin:
Then may he shoot rejoicing in innocency—
    from ambush or a safe distance;
Or he will beguile them, lay poison for them,
    keep no faith with them;
For what faith is there with that which cannot
    reckon hereafter,
Neither by itself, nor by another, nor by any
    residuum of ill consequences?
Surely, where weakness is utter, honour
    ceaseth.

Nay, I will do what is right in the eyes of him
    who can harm me,
And not in those of him who cannot call me
    to account.
Therefore yield me up thy pretty wings, O
    humming-bird!
Sing for me in a prison, O lark! Pay me thy
    rent, O widow! for it is mine.
Where there is reckoning there is sin,
And where there is no reckoning sin is not.

Surely this poem reveals the depth of insight and
morality, by the light of which the darkness seen

by the seer is cast. Is not what Butler writes here the truth of the morality practised by the vast majority of men, including those who regard themselves and are regarded as religious, as Christian? We glimpse here the hidden light of Butler's soul. He was most tender-hearted, considerate of the feelings even of the humblest creatures. In medicine he followed homœopathy, and I think it was significantly from humanitarian motives. At heart Butler felt that one must not be responsible for the inflicting of any pain that can honourably be avoided.

In 1876 Butler's father wrote to him inquiring about his financial status. Butler replied with a polite refusal to accept any help from him, if this should happen to be the object of the inquiry.

Writing to Miss Savage about his biological theory, Butler said:

The theory frightens me—it is so far-reaching and subversive—it oppresses me and I take panics that there cannot really be any solid truth in it; but I have been putting down anything that it seems to me can be urged against it with as much force as if I were a hostile reviewer, and really cannot see that I have a leg to stand upon when I pose as an objector. Still, do what I can, I am oppressed and frightened. I have had to read a sermon of Bishop Butler's again (author of *The Analogy*). And here again I am oppressed and frightened when I reflect that such a poor creature as he should have achieved so great and so lasting an influence.

As Festing Jones says—surely with real insight—" probably Heatherley's operated beneficially by taking him off his literary work and providing a place of quiet rest and meditation." But Butler's case was one in which the conscious mind was set on one thing, becoming a successful painter of pictures, while behind this his mind was achieving along another line. Butler thought nothing of selling pictures, it was not the idea of sacrilege that prevented that, but his books were things that had got to be written.

A sidelight on this inner disharmony is thrown by a letter from Miss Savage, in which she anticipated recent psychology: " Why do you paint in your dreams? Because you are vexed and angry with yourself for not being able to paint in the daytime? " She constantly tried to ease his mental tension with her jokes, as when she wrote that she had said of her enemy that " she combined the harmlessness of the serpent with the wisdom of the dove." While she was doing this she was suffering from cancer. Butler was absorbed in his own affairs and was not sufficiently aware of what she was enduring. His obtuseness—as it seemed to him later—was to cause him bitter pain. He hurt her without intending to, and she forgave him. Her conduct to him was monumentally good.

Beneath the surface there was still more excuse for Butler. He left a description of his state of mind at this time:

What with Pauli, who let me share and share down to the last drop of the capital I was now eating—nay, he had the lion's share—what with seeing ruin approaching and finding both literature and painting to be broken reeds so far as selling was concerned; what with relations between myself and my father and the really great anxiety that *Life and Habit* was to me, I was not myself.

He borrowed on every penny of capital he possessed. He gave himself a two months' holiday every summer and as many smaller outings as he could get. He believed that this was necessary.

In 1877 he wrote, " I am working at my book again regularly and go to the Brit. Mus. Reading Room every Monday, Wednesday and Friday from ten till one. I like it immensely, and wonder why I never went there before. I sit at letter B (B for Butler), or, if I cannot get there, at letter C." Presently we find him writing, " I believe the book will succeed and am now thoroughly absorbed in it. I suspect, now that I have found out the Museum, I shall never be long without a new book on hand and shall let them off pretty rapidly." Thus ended his career as a painter. Between 1869 and 1876 some half-dozen pictures by him had been hung at the Royal Academy Exhibitions. But now he turned definitely to literature, although he painted later as an amateur. He continued to spend his mornings in the British Museum, writing, until his death.

Great was the ardour with which he now pursued his vision which was the theme of *Life and Habit*, great were the excitement of the chase, the dizzying hopes and fears incident upon his theories. His anxiety was twofold, for it seemed necessary that the book should justify itself both intellectually and financially. The strain affected him so powerfully that while he was writing *Life and Habit* (and for a whole year afterwards) he was unable to breathe properly.

In September, 1877, Francis Darwin called on Butler. In conversation he said that the theory that had pleased him more than any he had lately met with was one referring all the phenomena of life or heredity to memory. Butler said that that was precisely what he was doing. Darwin then said that Ray Lankester had written a letter to *Nature* on the subject, but he could not remember exactly when. Butler said that he would not read it as his book was too far advanced and it might unsettle him. He wrote, however, afterwards and asked Francis Darwin if he could give him some idea as to when Lankester's letter had appeared. Francis Darwin did not send the reference. Butler wrote to him preparing him for the fact that he had come to differ fundamentally from his (Francis Darwin's) father and explaining how he had come to do so. In this letter he wrote:

Nothing would surprise me less than to see something sprung upon me in reviews and answers which cuts the ground completely from under me; and, of course, I neither expect nor give quarter in a philosophical argument. We want to get on the right side; and neither your father, I take it, nor I care two straws how we get on the right side as long as we get there. Neither do we want half refutations nor beatings about the bush. We want to come to an understanding as to what is

true and what false as soon as possible; and
we know well that we score more by retracting
after we have been deeply committed, than by
keeping to our original course when a new light
has been presented to us.

As we have seen, Butler was so deeply in
earnest about his book that it actually affected
his breathing. For the very reason that he was
so deeply in earnest, he was so much the more on
his guard against didacticism, which, as he had
said, " is a sin that doth so easily beset me." It
was this that led him to put at the beginning of
the book, " I have no wish to instruct, and not
much to be instructed; my aim is simply to
entertain and interest the numerous class of
people who, like myself, know nothing of science,
but who enjoy speculating and reflecting (not too
deeply) upon the phenomena around them."
Butler formally disowned any academic status.
He thought he could appeal to the educated
public, that they would judge his book on its
merits. Therefore he would write to interest
that public, introduce humour, and so on.
Butler's French lady friend had said of him,
" Il sait tout, il ne sait rien." Here was the
classical instance. In fact, he knew all about
what he was writing of, while he was childishly
unaware of the facts that the " experts " are

almost all obsessed by conventions in their own circles, that the educated public is almost entirely obsessed by the experts, and that the chance of a book on a "technical" subject being dealt with on its merits is of the smallest.

He did know that important views were accepted, on the authority of scientists, which were untrue. So he put on his title-page quotations from Lucian which he rendered as follows:

"We are all terribly afraid of them."

"Lay it well, therefore, before Jupiter, that if he will not bring these men of science to their proper bearings, I can stay here no longer."

"It shall be done," I answered.

Life and Habit was published on Butler's birthday, December 4, 1877.

"LIFE AND HABIT"

One of the great difficulties in effecting a synthesis of experience is the contradiction of the apparently mechanical character of the physical universe, on the one hand, and the sense of freedom we associate with life, on the other. In our own persons, we are told by scientists, or some of them, we are governed by physiological laws that are mechanical, as distinct from vital, in their nature. Now Butler pointed out that, in the functioning of our bodies, a large number of functionings that are apparently mechanical are really due to habits that have become stereotyped, and he drew attention to the fact that human functionings can be classified as follows:

I. We are most conscious of, and have most control over, such habits as speech, the upright position, the arts and sciences—which are acquisitions peculiar to the human race, are always acquired after birth, and are not common to ourselves and any ancestor who had not become entirely human.

II. We are less conscious of, and have less control over, eating, drinking, swallowing, breathing, seeing and hearing—which were acquisitions of our pre-human ancestry, and for which we had provided ourselves with all the necessary apparatus before human history began, but which are, biologically speaking, recent.

III. We are most unconscious of, and have least control over, our digestion and circulation—powers possessed even by our invertebrate ancestry and, even biologically speaking, of extreme antiquity.

Taking one of these functionings, breathing, Butler pointed out that it is an action apparently acquired after birth—with some little hesitation and difficulty, but in a time seldom longer than ten minutes or a quarter of an hour. There would seem to be a disproportion here, he says, between, on the one hand, the extreme intricacy of the process and, on the other, the shortness of the time taken to acquire the practice, the ease and unconsciousness with which its exercise is continued from the moment of acquisition. Butler says that it looks like the repetition of a performance by one who has done it very often before, but who requires just a little prompting to set him off, on getting which the whole familiar routine presents itself before him and he repeats his task by rote. Butler's argument is that the baby learnt to breathe in the persons of its ancestors right back in remote biological times when they were learning to breathe on leaving the sea for life on land; that there has been continuity with each and all of its ancestors, through whom this accumulation of powers has gone on; and that each individual has been repeating the process of learning to breathe whenever it finds itself in the stage in the recapitulation at which learning to breathe is called for; but the innumerable repetitions have facilitated the process enormously; indeed, it is repeated in epitome merely.[1]

[1] Butler apparently did not know that in the earlier Church, the authorities held that the human soul is passed on from father to son. Augustine was led to confess that he could discover by neither study nor prayer nor any process of reasoning how the doctrine of original sin could be defended on the supposition of the creation of souls. Truly, the whirligig of time brings in its revenges.

Learning to breathe is only one of the functionings referred to above, and they are, in turn representative of vastly more. But they belong to a historical sequence. Learning to breathe, for example, is only one incident in the operation of the Law of Recapitulation—the law that each individual living thing in its growth exhibits features which were characteristic of stages in the ancestry, more or less in the order in which they were acquired.

There is a great accumulation of evidence that the ovum and spermatozoon carry over an epitome of the ancestral memories of the whole of their ancestries. Only, great repetition is necessary for evident inheritance, and then the inheritance is below the threshold of consciousness. The efforts of the individuals in the ancestry and their results have been merged into one series : experiences have become experience unconscious and stereotyped, yet alive.

When a series of events is impressed on the memory by repetition, one starts at the beginning of the series normally, so that the earlier in the series the data are, the more secure and stereotyped they are because they have been the more often repeated, and they have become unconscious in corresponding degree. In learning any

series of acts, we are at first very conscious of
them, but with repetition we become less and
less conscious of them until at last the series
becomes unconscious. This, according to
Butler, is the explanation of the fact noted above,
that we are most conscious of and have most
control over functionings that are peculiar to
the human race and are always apparently
acquired after birth; that we are less conscious
of, and have less control over functionings that
were prehuman but still, biologically speaking,
recent; and that we are most unconscious of,
and have least control over, functionings that are,
even biologically speaking, of extreme antiquity.
The infant becomes conscious as he emerges to
less often repeated experiences. In repeating in
our minds in the usual way a series—for example,
a list of events in chronological order—we find
that there are units or patches that, for some
reason or other, stand out. So in Recapitulation
patches stand out.

An act leaves some trace in the actor. By
repetition this accumulates. The trace becomes
a tendency. As regards the development of a
new character, in the biological sense, all we
know is that by repetition of the action concerned
the biological character develops.

The recapitulation is adjusted to requirements

revealed in the later experience of the creature, so that the formation of the structure to be required can take place before the structure is actually required.

In every individual living thing which is of protoplasm, the life begins, so far as we can see, in the form of a protoplasmic cell and passes rapidly and in " unconscious consciousness " along the mnemic path of habit worn smooth by the repetitions of countless generations. In the case of bi-sexual animals, the habit of the union of two cells, male and female, is essential to the further development. In every individual living thing as it grows, the life, when it comes to those parts of the mnemic course of the ancestry which are tracts rather than a path worn unified, becomes conscious; still, however, retaining the various strata of " unconscious consciousness " which merge into each other, as in breathing, digesting, etc.

A sequence of individuals, a species, may, initiatively, solve problems of living or of adding to its life. It may come into a condition of contentment and cease to progress. It is capacity for new adaptations that counts— not so much the new situation as the new adapting, whether in reaction to environment or initiatively.

Butler's method of presentation, from the point of view of getting his views believed in by a large public, suffered and suffers from a defect which is probably the result of his loneliness and the meticulousness of his introspection. What is amazing naïveté, in view of Butler's serious expectation that the book would be taken up, is great charm from the more literary point of view:

In the outset, however, I would wish most distinctly to disclaim for these pages the smallest pretensions to scientific value, originality, or even to accuracy of more than a very rough and ready kind—for unless a matter is true enough to stand a good deal of misrepresentation, its truth is not of a very robust order, and the blame will rather lie with its own delicacy if it be crushed, than with the carelessness of the crusher.

This is the attitude of the really great man. It is magnificent, but it is not war. But even this was exceeded:

Above all things, let no unwary reader do me the injustice of believing in *me*. In that I write at all I am among the damned. If he must believe in anything, let him believe in the music of Handel, the painting of Giovanni Bellini, and in the thirteenth chapter of St. Paul's First Epistle to the Corinthians.

In Butler's style of presentation is what Shaw found in George Henry Lewes (and what he himself has done)—" . . . exacting all this from himself, and then expressing his most laboured conclusions with a levity that gave them the air of being the unpremeditated whimsicalities of a man who had perversely taken to writing for the sake of the jest latent in his own outrageous unfitness for it."

Butler believed that people would be disarmed by this modesty and would perceive the truth and importance of what he was writing the book about. Like many another original and able man, he exaggerated the intelligence and independence of the intelligentsia. He did not realize that it is dominated by conventions and that a book to be conventionally approved must be written in the conventional way—with but little departure from it, at all events—that this is true in respect of the intelligentsia and not only of the academic. And hence we find him writing that his book " is intended for the general public only, with whom I believe myself to be in harmony."

He was too great a humanist to let scientific interest exclude humanism:

No man is a great hypocrite until he has left off knowing that he is a hypocrite. The great hypocrites of the world are almost invariably

under the impression that they are among the
few really honest people to be found. In like
manner, the most perfect humour and irony is
generally quite unconscious.

This he illustrates by pointing out that Milton
did not know he was a humorist when he spent
his honeymoon in composing a treatise on
divorce. This sort of thing, though most wel-
come to a Butlerian, was a confusing of the
scientific argument of the book. From time
to time this humanism finds expression. For
example, his reaction against Victorianism:

Truly if there is one who cannot find himself
in the same room with the life and letters of an
earnest person without being instantly unwell,
the same is a just man and perfect in all his ways.

Or anon he will coin a great epigram :

The greatest men are they who are most
uncertain in spite of certainty, and at the same
time most certain in spite of uncertainty.

Or again he will argue that grace is the seal of
accomplishment:

Of the pioneers, on the other hand, some are
agreeable people while others are ugly, rude
and disagreeable people, very progressive, it
may be, but very aggressive to boot. With
the pioneers it is *sic vos non vobis*.

And grace is best, for where grace is, love is

not distant. Grace! the old pagan ideal whose charm even unlovely Paul could not withstand, but, as the legend tells us, his soul fainted within him, his heart misgave him, and, standing alone on the seashore at dusk, he " troubled deaf heaven with his bootless cries," his thin voice pleading for grace after the flesh. The waves came in one after another, the seagulls cried together after their kind, the wind rustled among the dried canes upon the sandbanks, and there came a voice from heaven saying, " Let my grace be sufficient for thee." Whereon, failing of the thing itself, he stole the word and strove to crush its meaning to the measure of his own limitations. But the true grace, with her groves and high places, and troups of young men and maidens crowned with flowers and singing of love and youth and wine—the true grace he drove out into the wilderness—high up, it may be, into Piora, and into such-like places. Happy they who harboured her in her ill-report.

The introduction of Piora is characteristic of Butler. He loved the place: he wanted to immortalize it: and he cared not that it was not well known.

Although Butler did not see how his book would be damned by convention, he did see the domination of the herd instinct even in modern and scientific society and coined a fine epigram to express it: "Sanction sanctifieth and fashion fashioneth." By his insight he saw contemporaneously that the superstition of his time was science of his time. People do not hold a superstition believing it to be a superstition. The commonly accepted, the obvious, often hides a deeper truth.

The truth is, according to Butler, that all life comes from within, although truth, goodness and beauty are objective too. Only, the assimilation of the true, the good, and the beautiful is relative to the assimilator, and to be assimilated heartily, a thing must be neither too familiar nor too unfamiliar. The realization of the true, the good and the beautiful depends on the vigour of the life within. Many lives are rendered futile by the fallacy that by not coming to a decision, one avoids harm:

As with painting or music, so with life and politics, let every man be fully persuaded in his own mind, for decision with wrong will be commonly better than indecision—I had almost added, with right and a firm purpose with risk than an infirm one with temporary exemption from disaster.

Things that really matter can be done only with the help of an inward desire to learn. If a being wants to learn or to improve generally, he will

do so in spite of any hindrance till in time he
becomes very different from what he was originally. If he does not wish to learn or improve,
he will not do so. If he feels he has the power,
he will wish; or if he wishes, he will begin to
think he has the power.

One of Butler's strong points, however, is
that his advocacy of a particular view does not
blind him to the contributions of competing
views. In the present instance, for example,
although he stresses the importance in evolution
of the desire of the being, he recognizes that
" chance " can be exceedingly " lucky ":

Occasionally a blunder might prove a happy
accident, as happens not infrequently with
painters, musicians, chemists, and inventors;
or sometimes a creature with exceptional
powers of memory or reflection would make
his appearance in this race or that. We all
profit by our accidents as well as by our more
cunning contrivances, so that analogy would
point in the direction of thinking that many of
the most happy thoughts in the animal and
vegetable kingdoms were originated much as
certain discoveries among ourselves. These
would be originally blind variations, though,
even so, probably less blind than we think, if
we could only know the whole truth.

There can be no doubt that Butler anticipated the discovery of the unconscious by Freud and others. He saw, for example, that virtues are largely sublimations: "Not less, in all probability than a full twenty per cent. of all the courage and good nature now existing in the world derives its origin, at no very distant date, from a desire to appear courageous and good-natured."

His final position is that all truth, including scientific truth, is symbolism; there is no *absolute* truth available, but truth is available in the sense that there is real art: life at its highest, man at his highest, is an artist revealing the highest experience to which he has attained[1]: the

---

[1] In *The Times* for April 4, 1934, appeared the following letter:

Sir,—Your article of April 2 reminds me of a suggestion I threw out many years ago at a Norfolk farm auction lunch, namely, that farming is an art as well as a science.

The mysterious something which enables a man to be continuously successful in farming must, to some extent, lie in his power of forecasting the future, whether it be the weather or trend of prices. Such a man will top-dress his corn sparingly or abundantly according to his sense of what sort of summer will ensue, he will harvest his crops to the best advantage, cutting and carrying in the nick of time; he will buy or sell stock according to his sense of coming values, and his uninspired neighbours would be wise to follow his example, though he could not justify his action by logical arguments.

There must be many degrees in this sensitiveness, from the man who is never wrong to the man who is rarely right. The word "art" is perhaps not quite appropriate. "Religion" would be nearer, but it is liable to be misunderstood. The quality I recognize is independent of climate or creed and has been observed in all past ages. It applies to all walks in life, but is specially noticeable in agriculture.

Yours faithfully,

Athenaeum Club.   LAWRENCE G. JONES.

individual strokes and forms are not absolutely true but the integration of the work of art expresses valid truth.

In spite of all his camouflage, Butler was deeply in earnest in his quest for the way out of determinism:

> Will the reader bid me wake with him to a world of chance and blindness? Or can I persuade him to dream with me of a more living faith than either he or I had as yet conceived as possible? As I have said, reason points remorselessly to an awakening, but faith and hope still beckon to the dream.

These are the last words of the book.

The dedication of *Life and Habit* is as follows:

> This work is inscribed to Charles Paine Pauli, Esq., barrister-at-law, in acknowledgment of his invaluable criticism of the proof-sheets of this and of my previous books and in recognition of an old and well-tried friendship.

Surely Antony's response to Enobarbus was here matched in life by Butler.

It was in a letter to him about *Life and Habit* that Miss Savage worked off one of her best little jokes: " there are a great many hard words in the book: but I don't mind them, for I have a dictionary which I bought two years ago as I wished to read *Daniel Deronda* in the original."

Butler sent his father a notice of *Life and Habit* from *The Standard*. His father replied that he had made a point of not reading any of his son's books except *A First Year in Canterbury Settlement*.

Butler made a series of notes for a volume II of *Life and Habit*, among which occur the following:

the one true Catholic Church of all amiable people.

The public want a straight tip for the purchase of a little Holy Ghost cheap.

The prophets entered into a life which has not yet failed them because they said what they had to say without fear of what man could do to them.

The poet and the prophet show us their hearts.

"EVOLUTION OLD AND NEW"

Butler looked up the article in *Nature* by Ray Lankester which Francis Darwin had told him referred to a paper advancing the memory theory of heredity and found that it dealt with the Presidential Address given to the Imperial Academy of Science at Vienna by Professor Hering "On Memory as a Universal Function of Organized Matter." It is noteworthy that Ray Lankester accepted the view of Hering and that

this fact was so little commented on at the time
or since and that Butler did not comment on it.
Hering's was a very remarkable lecture, revealing
the insight of genius, and it is a striking coinci-
dence that it gave (in brief outline) the main
doctrine at which Butler independently arrived.
Butler wrote to *The Athenaeum* (February 8,
1878) calling attention to the lecture.

In the words of his biographer, he " re-read
The Origin of Species, and in the third edition he
found a ' brief but imperfect ' sketch of the
progress of opinion on the subject of the origin
of species prior to the publication of the first
edition. This led him to read each of the
writers mentioned in the sketch and he was
astonished at the completeness of the theory of
evolution contained in the works of Buffon
(between 1749 and 1788); in the *Zoonomia* of Dr.
Erasmus Darwin (1794); and in the writings of
Lamarck (between 1801 and 1831). He was
more astonished when he remembered that *The
Origin of Species* had left him under the impression
that evolution and natural selection were prac-
tically the same thing." That is to say, he was
staggered to find that the whole theory of
evolution had been fully enunciated three or four
times before Charles Darwin and, not only so,
but in a form recognizing the action of mind,

intelligence, purpose. Butler felt that this was so important that he must write a book about it.

One of Butler's first rewards on reading Erasmus Darwin was the following passage:

> Owing to the imperfection of language, the offspring is termed a new animal; but is, in truth, a branch or elongation of the parent, since a part of the embryon animal is or was a part of the parent and, therefore, in strict language, cannot be said to be entirely new at the time of its production, and, therefore, it may retain some of the habits of the parent system.

Anyone who has read *Life and Habit* attentively immediately recognizes here that Erasmus Darwin put into words almost the same as Butler's the very ideas that Butler subsequently discovered for himself. This was the first foreshadowing of the unity of parent and offspring and of unconscious habit that Butler had been able to find.

To him it was monstrous that the world had not been told that the whole theory of evolution had been fully enunciated three or four times, from Buffon onward, before Charles Darwin, and especially as these pioneers of the theory of evolution were so importantly superior to Charles Darwin and his contemporaries in the very particulars in which they differed from them. To Butler it was the simple issue of knave or fool. He could not believe that ignorance and immersion in technical detail might be the comparatively innocent causes of a very real and important neglect. He therefore charged Darwin with having consciously refrained from giving his predecessors, including his own grandfather, the credit due to them.

About three months after it was announced that Butler was writing about Erasmus Darwin, it was announced that Charles Darwin was going to write about Erasmus Darwin.

Evolution Old and New was published in 1879. It has been described by Professor MacBride as the most brilliant history of the theory of evolution. In publishing it, Butler introduced the innovation of numbering his books as " Op. 4 " and so on.

In 1879 in *The Examiner* Butler ran a correspondence, extending from February till May, purporting to arise from " An Earnest Clergyman " who, after having taken orders, and who had a wife and children, discovered that he did not believe orthodox Christianity. He discusses the position most thoroughly and ably from the various points of view.

In one of these letters he says:

it became plain to me that the Christ-idea,
like every living form of faith, or living faith
of form, had descended with modification,
and, what is worse, through insufficient
breeding, it had reverted to a remote ancestor
and resumed feral characteristics.

"GOD THE KNOWN AND GOD THE UNKNOWN"

In 1879 he published a series of articles in
The Examiner entitled " God the Known and God
the Unknown, an Eirenicon." The thesis was
that the power within, whence come all the
phenomena of organic life, may be denominated
" God ":

We enthrone him upon the wings of birds,
on the petals of flowers, on the faces of our
friends, and upon whatever we most delight
in of all that lives upon the earth. We can
express our love and have it expressed to us in
return—in the caress bestowed on horse and
dog, and kisses upon the lips of those we
love.

Incidentally, in these papers Butler touched
deep philosophy:

It has been said, " *Tempora mutantur, nos et
mutamur in illis.*"[1] The passage would have

[1] The sentence occurs in an obscure seventeenth-century writer
called Borbonius: but he wrote, better, *omnia*.

been no less true had it stood, " *Nos mutamur et tempora mutantur in nobis.*"

He explains "sports" by a psychological explanation:

Great thoughts must present themselves for capture of their own free will, or be taken after a little coyness only. They are like wealth and power, which, if a man is not born to them, are the more likely to take him the more he has restrained himself from an attempt to snatch them. They hanker after those only who have tamed their nearer thoughts. But vigorous minds will harbour vigorous thoughts only, or such as bid fair to become so: the mind is prepared by preliminary modification of itself.

According to Butler, at this stage in his thought —in the words of Mrs. Stillman, " God is the Life Force, a God not perfect and complete, not omnipresent, omniscient, or infinite but vastly powerful and resourceful, ceaselessly aspiring and changing, a God whose possibilities are unforseeable, unknown even to himself, at each step of the way knowing only the next step, and proceeding by infinitesimal progressions, by trial and error, achievement, failure, wisdom and folly along the road of adventure and memory that has led from scarcely sentient slime to the complex organism of human being and human society. He thought that there might be a still greater and an unknown God looming behind this one, composed of lesser Gods, as our God is composed of the living forms of the earth and as we are composed of the cells of our own bodies."[1]

In these articles Butler drew a sharp line of division between the organic and the inorganic, but soon after, he came to see that this was wrong.

In 1879 was published " *Erasmus Darwin* by Ernst Krause. Translated from the German by W. S. Dallas, with a preliminary notice by Charles Darwin." The book was stated by Darwin to be a translation of an article by Krause which had been published in a German magazine in February. It contained the sentence, " Erasmus Darwin's system was in itself a most significant first step in the path of knowledge which his grandson has opened for us; but the wish to revive it at the present day, as has actually been seriously attempted, shows a weakness of thought and a mental anachronism that no one can envy."

Butler sent to Germany for the number of the magazine containing Krause's article and began to learn German. When he saw it, he found

[1] Stillman, *Samuel Butler*, p. 210.

that the article did not contain any of the last six pages of the book, and that there were other points of difference which showed, as it seemed to him, that the article must have been altered in view of *Evolution Old and New*.

Butler wrote to Darwin. Darwin replied that the article had been altered, but explained that he had attached no importance to this: now he was sorry he had not said so in the book: if there should be a reprint, he would say so. (He naturally did not mention that, in sending *Evolution Old and New* to Krause, he had written that he hoped that Krause would "not expend much powder and shot on Mr. Butler, for he really is not worthy of it. His book is merely ephemeral.")

Butler was not satisfied with Darwin's reply and wrote to *The Athenaeum*. Darwin consulted Huxley, who advised no reply. In the Darwin circle Butler's letter was considered " so ungentle-manlike as not to deserve an answer." (As to this, the letter has been published and anyone can judge for himself.) Francis Darwin and some of his brothers thought that a reply ought to be sent.

What Butler felt to be unjust was that, although the article had been altered in view of *Evolution Old and New*, it had been given forth on

the authority of Charles Darwin that Butler's
view of the teaching of Erasmus Darwin had
been anticipated and was worthless. To Butler
it seemed, surely naturally, that here was confirmation of the issue *qua* Charles Darwin of
knave or fool. As is not seldom the case, the
latter appeared the more incredible of the two.

Butler, having learnt German in order to read
Krause's original, turned to read Hering's lecture
and he wrote to Hering asking his permission to
publish a translation.

In a letter to a friend written at this time is a
very remarkable passage:

I have finally made up my mind that there
is no hard and fast line to be drawn, and that
every molecule of matter is full of will and
consciousness and that the motion of the stars
in space is voluntary and of design on their
parts. I find a passage in Walt Whitman which
will serve for my title-page; it runs: " I do
not doubt that the orbs and systems of orbs
ply their swift spirits through the air on
purpose." It is so; and I think I can make it
pretty clear, too. As for the Newtonian
system, there is a horrible screw loose in it.
I did not find it out, but, when I came across

it, it was a very clear case; and Jones and my
cousin see it too, and so will you when I show
it to you; and nothing but volition will get it
straight.

This sounds remarkable when we recall that a
few years ago the Newtonian system was super-
seded by a Copernican revolution and that Edding-
ton has argued for volition in the unit of matter.

Butler had published *Evolution Old and New*
with David Bogue. Bogue now offered him
£100 for a book of Italian travel, with illustrations, and Butler set to work.

Butler and Pauli had been consuming Butler's
remaining capital and he was earning nothing:
he was sliding steadily down to complete insol-
vency. About this time he made inquiries
about the market value of the Whitehall reversion,
which he knew would reach his father's ears.
" A voluminous and painful correspondence
ensued," and it became necessary for Butler to
disclose to his father in detail the miserable
adventure of the lost capital and the unlosable
Pauli. Canon Butler made private inquiries
about Pauli and was told that he was making
£1,000 a year, but Pauli, on being questioned by
Butler, vehemently denied this. Butler wrote

to his father giving a complete account of his
financial transactions, including the sums he had
spent on Pauli and in repaying Heatherley and
others for the stock he had induced them to buy
and once more asking him to make the reversion
absolute so that he could borrow on it.   This
his father refused to do and, after many letters
had passed between them and the permanent
bitterness between them was again brought to
the boiling-point, it was finally agreed that
Butler's father would make him an allowance
of £300 a year, with the proviso that Butler
should do nothing more for Pauli, and that
anything he made by writing should be deducted
from the £300.   Further, Canon Butler informed
him that he should have only a life interest in the
greater part of what he intended to leave him.
Butler wrote to his father that he considered this
" the heaviest blow a father can inflict upon a
son " but which he felt incapable of discussing
with him.

Here we see tragedy in real life: the father
thinking of his son as the black sheep of the
family, not knowing that the day would come
when the world would regard his son as the
success and himself as the black sheep.   And yet
surely, from his father's point of view, Butler
was not to be trusted with capital.

H

Early in 1880 there was introduced to Butler
H. S. Tuke, the painter, and Butler got to like
him very much. Butler wrote him a series of
letters in this year giving his advice on the subject
of marriage.   On July 12 he wrote:

Don't marry any woman without being so
much in love with her that you feel you would
rather be made into mincemeat than not marry
her.   Even though you may have proposed,
break the match off (it is the kindest thing to
do, in the long run) rather than this. This is
how Paget felt to Miss Farr, and the match is
and will be a happy one. If you feel like this
to any woman, you can hardly marry her too
soon, but anything short of this is, I believe,
one of the gravest crimes of which a man can
well be guilty.

This is rather a simple matter to write about,
but I sometimes think you hear a great deal
of trash talked by people older than yourself
who do not know what they ought to know,
and I am anxious about you.   I have no right
to be anxious about you, but I certainly am.

Do not answer this, or take further steps
about our meeting in Italy, unless you approve
of the advice it contains.   If you do approve
of it, I will come any distance to see you:
if you do not, I can be of no service to you.

P.S. You may perhaps approve the substance of what I have written but not approve of my having written it: in that case I shall be so well content with your acceptance of the substance that I shall be at any rate in some measure consoled.

Bystanders sometimes see more of a drama than the chief actors in it.

On July 28 he wrote to Tuke:

I have no business to think such a lot of you as we all of us do, or to meddle with things that don't concern me. Still, you were good enough to answer my letter. . . . You are evidently not only not in love—well, you are evidently not one particle in love. The whole is a got-up thing. Some people have played hard to catch you : others who take precious good care to keep out of the mess themselves have egged you on till you have got into a false position.

A man's first duty is to himself, and if he fails in it he will fail in duty to the very ones whom he is most trying to observe duty towards. If he fails in so great a duty to himself as that of not sacrificing himself for life, I for one am heartily sorry for him, but I cannot help him. No sensible man who reads the note you sent me can doubt that the sooner you break away, the better both for yourself and the heroine.

If you are in any difficulty whatever, money or what not, through which you find yourself hindered, and wish to see me, let me know and I will not be long in coming. Otherwise either come and see me, or let us meet half way.

P.S.   I trust I did not use the word " frank." You have put it in inverted commas. It makes me sick.

On August 15 he wrote to Tuke:

To me you seem to have been the victim of one of the most unprincipled attempts I remember to have seen tried on unsuspecting innocence, and to have been advised by friends who were none the less mischievous for the blindness and stupidity to which their mischief was owing; but you have been very stupid and weak yourself too.   If I thought you were in love, I would not say one word of this, but you and I well know that you are nothing of the kind, and on this the whole thing becomes a miserable and contemptible falsehood, a more specious, but less easily intelligible self abuse.   Horrible to think of.

I don't care so much what you do now that you have your eyes open, as I trust you have, but I ventured on a great liberty because I thought I was almost the only person I knew of who would have the impudence to do it, and I felt it ought to be done by someone.[1]

In 1880 Butler published

"UNCONSCIOUS MEMORY"

in which he gave his translation of Hering's lecture and his own comments thereon. An important point in Hering which impressed Butler is his theory of the part played by vibrations in Nature. Butler also dealt with von Hartmann's theory of the unconscious in this book, but Butler was prejudiced against von Hartmann, and did him less than justice.

Miss Savage in a letter to Butler in 1881 told him a story about himself: " One day when I was going to the gallery, a very hot day, I remember, I met you on the shady side of Berners Street, eating cherries out of a basket. Like your Italian friends, you were perfectly silent with content, and you handed the basket to me as I was passing, without saying a word. I pulled out a handful and went on my way rejoicing without saying a word either."

In 1881 Canon Butler suddenly and without further pressure from Butler granted what the

[1] These letters are taken from the biography of Tuke.

latter had repeatedly asked for in the matter of
the reversion. He made it absolute, and Butler
at once gave up the allowance from his father,
invested the money he borrowed on the reversion
in leaseholds, and renewed his allowance to Pauli,
disregarding the fact that the latter had survived
eighteen months without his assistance.

Festing Jones took scarlet fever. Butler sat
up with him every night while it was at its worst.
It was particularly inconvenient for him to spend
the night in an arm-chair just then as he was
suffering from a cracked rib. He was at this
time very hard at work on both text and illustrations for the book of Italian travel com-
missioned by Bogue which emerged as *Alps and
Sanctuaries*. When it came to publication, Bogue
went back on his commission to Butler, and the
latter had to publish it at his own expense.

"ALPS AND SANCTUARIES"

This is the most delightful of Butler's books
and is the one to be recommended as an introduction to him. The illustrations are from
drawings made by him from his sketches in
colour and a few by Festing Jones, with the
figures inserted by Gogin. Gogin etched the
frontispiece from one of Butler's sketches. All
of these are most charming. Butler introduced

passages of music as illustrations, of which practice Mr. R. A. Streatfeild, who was by way of being an authority on music, wrote, " He deserves the credit due to a pioneer for the happy audacity of his discovery, often exemplified in his books, that scenery can be described in terms of music."

Butler once said that a man's holiday is his garden, and the book is of his holidays and his garden, which was Italy. It is as if he were talking to you on holiday with him in Italy.

It is his talk, then, that is the book, his *obiter dicta*. He talks about what interests him and seems important to him. In art, for example, he says, what matters is not technique but the communication of the spirit of the artist. The supreme artist is Handel: " he is as much above Shakespeare as Shakespeare is above all others: ' there,' said Beethoven on his deathbed, pointing to the works of Handel, ' there is truth.' " If the medium of communication is a picture, the way to find out whether you like it is to ask yourself whether you would care to look at it if you were quite sure you were alone.

Anon he is talking about the rate at which inventions come:

Our inventions increase in geometrical

ratio. They are like living beings, each one
of which may become a parent of a dozen
others—some good and some ne'er-do-wells;
but they differ from animals and vegetables
inasmuch as they not only increase in geometrical ratio, but the period of their gestation
decreases in geometrical ratio also. . . . The
first period, from the chamois track to the
foot road, was one of millions of years; the
second, from the first foot-road to the Roman
military way, was one of many thousands; the
third, from the Roman to the mediaeval, was
perhaps a thousand; from the mediaeval to
the Napoleonic, five hundred; from the
Napoleonic to the railroad, fifty. What will
come next we know not, but it should come
within twenty years.

One of Butler's favourite doctrines was that a
man should be so sure of himself that he could
travesty the things most sacred to him. " Cross-
ing " was requisite in life. " I would send people
like Mr. Gladstone to attend Mr. Bradlaugh's
lectures in the forenoon, and the Grecian panto-
mime in the evening, two or three times every
winter." " I make it a practice to swallow a few
gnats a day lest I should come to strain at them
and so bolt camels." " All depends upon who
it is that is lying. One may steal a horse when

another may not look over a hedge."[1] "A man's safety lies in temper—in the power of fusing faith and reason, even when they appear most mutually destructive."

Some of the best writing on art is in this volume. Butler insisted that the best art was unself-conscious as art. "The illustrations to *Punch* are often as good as anything that can be imagined." Different ages have their own *forms* of art in which they excel. So long as Italian painters supplied pictures in demand and taught apprentices, making money out of them, Italian art was good; but with the rise of the academy of art, Italian art declined. Imitation of the mature is substituted for the student learning from mistakes. The student must do real work, with responsibility, not merely exercises.

It does not matter what a man does; so long as he does it with the attention which affection engenders, he will come to see his way to something else. After long waiting he will certainly find one door open, and go through it. He will say to himself that he can never find another. Yet by and by he will see that there is one small, unimportant door which he had overlooked, and he proceeds through this

[1] Festing Jones, in one of his books, gave a good instance: One driver flicks the horse's ears with his whip to annoy the horse; another, to relieve it from flies.

too. Then eventually his openings will become big enough.

Universities and academies are an obstacle to the finding of doors in later life: partly because they push young men too fast through doorways that the universities have provided, and so discourage the habit of being on the lookout for others; and partly because they do not take pains enough to make sure that their doors are *bona fide* ones. If, to change the metaphor, an academy has taken a bad shilling, it is seldom very scrupulous about trying to pass it on. It will stick to it that the shilling is a good one as long as the police will let it.

The secrets of success are affection for the pursuit chosen, a flat refusal to be hurried or to pass anything as understood which is not understood, and an obstinacy of character which shall make the student's friends find it less trouble to let him have his own way than to bend him to theirs.

Here are a few more of the *obiter dicta*:—first, a little passage of fine writing:

Seagulls, again, and the plaintive creatures that pity themselves on moorlands, as the plover and the curlew, or the birds that lift up their voices and cry at eventide when there

is an eager air blowing upon the mountains
and the last yellow in the sky is fading.

Butler's tenderness of heart is exemplified in
the following:

It is nearly a hundred years ago since that
little gray marmot's skin was tanned in the
Val Sesia; but the wretch will not lie quiet in
his grave; he walks, and has haunted me once
a month or so any time this ten years past.

Anon his humour comes up. He is describing
a picture of Christ before the Elders:

There is one man, I think he must have been
a broad churchman and have taken in the
Spectator. He is not prepared, he seems to say,
to deny that there is a certain element of truth
in what this young person has been saying, but
in all essential points it has been refuted over
and over again; he has seen these things come
and go often, etc.

Or again he has insight into the strong points in
the Roman Catholic Church:

We Protestants do not understand, nor take
any very great pains to understand, the Church
of Rome. If we did, we should find it to be
as much in advance of us in some respects as
it is behind us in others.

One final example of the miscellaneous wisdom
that is scattered through *Alps and Sanctuaries*:

Butler points out that some animals have not provided themselves with organs specially adapted to their tasks, but rely on skill in use; for example, the chamois and its feet.

Like its predecessors save *Erewhon*, *Alps and Sanctuaries* was a failure. Yet Butler wrote to Miss Savage: "I don't exactly see what it is that will bring about a reaction in my favour, but I feel pretty sure that it will come some day. The Darwin literary and scientific clique have done their utmost; they have no more cards to play; all that they can say or do is now done, and I think a gradual reaction may be hoped for with some confidence."

Butler got out a new edition of *Evolution Old and New* just as Charles Darwin died. He wrote a special preface about Darwin, which contains this passage:

It is unfortunately true that I believe Mr. Darwin to have behaved badly to me; this is too notorious to be denied; but at the same time I cannot be blind to the fact that no man can be a judge in his own case, and that, after all, Mr. Darwin may have been right and I wrong.

In an appendix Butler dealt with some of the

reviews. Grant Allen had written that Butler was a man of genius " with the unmistakable signet mark upon his forehead "; upon which Butler commented thus:

> I have been subjected to a good deal of obloquy and misunderstanding at one time or another, but the passage by Mr. Allen is the only one that has made me seriously uneasy about the prospects of my literary reputation.

Mr. Bernard Shaw has taken exception to this passage by Butler, but surely Butler clung to the view that he was far enough ahead of his time not to be recognized by his contemporaries. It is true that Grant Allen is reflected on, but he had given Butler good evidence to justify such reflection.

In the appendix Butler stood up to the pedants of science with complete courage, pointing out, for example, how ignorant they had been of the history of evolutionary theory until the publication of *Evolution Old and New* and how they had used the knowledge found therein without acknowledgment.

Butler added a second, most extraordinary, appendix on " Rome and Pantheism," actually offering an eirenicon to the Catholic Church on the basis of his pantheism. He was seeing centuries ahead and thinking it was to-morrow.

About the time of the publication of the second
" edition " of *Evolution Old and New*, Butler was
asked to give a lecture at the Working Men's
College, then in New Ormond Street, and he
accepted, and later he was asked to give others.
He was a success as a lecturer.

In 1883, when he was forty-seven, Butler
began to compose music. He and Jones soon
began to compose a mock-Handelian oratorio,
Narcissus.

BUTLER'S NOTEBOOKS

The first MS. volume of notes that Butler
kept ended in 1883. Early in life he had begun
to carry a notebook. Later he made it a practice
to copy such notes into larger books and to revise
them. This volume was begun in 1874. In the
preface that he came to write to the second volume,
he made observations that apply to all of them:

> I am alarmed at the triviality of many, the
> ineptitude of many, and the obvious untenable-
> ness of many that I should have done much
> better to destroy. They are not meant for
> publication.

A selection from Butler's notebooks was made
by Festing Jones and published in 1912. These
notes were not printed according to date of

composition. In *Further Selections from the Note-books of Samuel Butler* by A. T. Bartholomew, published in 1934, the arrangement according to date is kept. Here are some from the MS. volume which ended in 1883:

In art whatever has been once transcendent remains so, however much it be transcended later. All that is not transcendent dies and disappears—*exceptis excipiendis*.

Here is a Shakespearean fragment copied from a newspaper inquest report of 1858 or 1859:

" I say 'tis here, bring thy putty hither."

" Nay, but if it be not *here*, I will eat both thee and thy putty."

We profess to accept with thankfulness the the position of being God's sheep, yet few lambs are allowed to become full grown and it is not intended that any should die a natural death. A sheep's *raison d'être* is to be fleeced as often as possible, and then to have its throat cut. Uriah the Hittite, if his own life had been spared, would no doubt have sat down to the little ewe lamb which he carried so tenderly in his bosom, and dined off it with much satis-faction; and when, again, we see pictures of our Saviour with sheep behind him, and a lamb in his bosom, we should remember that

the matter will not end there. If a shepherd
caressing a lamb is a fair statement of the case,
a cat playing with a mouse should be hardly
less so. We may be asked to bless the grass,
the sunshine, and our fellow sheep, but can
we reasonably be expected to bless the butcher?
Is it not time to drop that metaphor?

The case of a woman now stands thus.
Every one of her ancestors for millions and
millions of generations has been endowed
with sexual instinct, and has effectually grati-
fied it. For a longer time than our imagination
can realize there has been no link broken, and
hence no exception. The instinct has been
approved, confirmed, and made stronger in
each successive generation. Surely she in
whom it has been sanctioned may claim the
right to gratify it, should occasion serve.
" No," says Society to the unmarried woman
very sternly: " break the link, in your own
person; stem the current of that passion to
which both we and you owe our very being;
run counter to the course of things that has
led up to you; be indifferent to that which has
ranked next to life itself in the heart of every
mother from whom you are descended. If
you even attempt this more than Herculean
task seriously, we will not honour you, but will

laugh at you for an old maid; if, on the other
hand, you are disobedient, we will chase you
into the streets and call you infamous." And
then we are surprised that women are not at all
times exactly what we could wish.

When we go to art, we go for the most part
to be taken both into common life and out of
it.

Isaac offering up Abraham would, I imagine,
have been very wrong, no matter how plainly
God told Isaac to do it. Fancy Abraham
letting Isaac get him on to the mountain on
such a ridiculous pretence as this!

Jones telling me about a funeral said, " And
then a gentleman in a white surplice met us
at the gate and announced himself as the
Resurrection and the Life. A man looked
down into the grave when the body was
lowered, and said cheerfully ' It seems to be a
nice gravelly soil,' and then they all went
away."

Never do anything till you are sure that it
is the most important thing as yet left undone.

George Eliot cribbed her chapter on
machines in *Theophrastus Such* from *Erewhon*.
I ought to be highly flattered. In one year
I made Mr. Darwin write a book (*Erasmus
Darwin*), and George Eliot crib a chapter.

Some years ago when Lord Lytton and I wrote books anonymously about the same time, I do not think I got the worst of it.

About 1883 Butler wrote some autobiographical notes, among which he makes the following significant statements:

New ideas crowd in through the very process of expressing old ones.

I believe *Alps and Sanctuaries* and *Life and Habit* to be my two best books hitherto.

I wrote a few letters and articles in the *Examiner* during the spring of 1879, but soon came to the conclusion that journalistic literature was not my forte. I have written two short reviews of books in my life, and two only—the one was Mr. Leslie Stephen's *Essays in Freethinking and Plainspeaking*. The other was on the philosophy of Rosmini. I never wrote a magazine article nor an art criticism.

In 1883 Butler wrote another psalm:

"TO CRITICS AND OTHERS"

O Critics, cultured Critics!

Who will praise me after I am dead,

Who will see in me both more and less than I intended,

But who will swear that whatever it was it was all perfectly right:

You will think you are better than the people who, when I was alive, swore that whatever I did was wrong

And damned my books for me as fast as I could write them;

But you will not be better, you will be just the same, neither better nor worse,

And you will go for some future Butler as your fathers have gone for me.

Oh! How I should have hated you!

But you, Nice People!

Who will be sick of me because the critics thrust me down your throats,

But who would take me willingly enough if you were not bored about me,

Or if you could have the cream of me— and surely this should suffice:

Please remember that, if I were living, I should be upon your side.

And should hate those who imposed me either on myself or others;

Therefore, I pray you, neglect me, burlesque me, boil me down, do whatever you like with me,

But do not think that, if I were living, I should not aid and abet you.

There is nothing that even Shakespeare

would enjoy more than a good burlesque of
Hamlet.[1]

In 1885 Miss Savage died. There can be no
doubt that Butler was fortunate indeed in
having had her as a woman friend with a
mind so well attuned to his most unusual
one. After her death he could not bear to
touch his novel, although he always wanted to
rewrite it.

"THE WAY OF ALL FLESH"

The title as settled by Butler was *Ernest Pontifex, or The Way of All Flesh, a Story of English
Domestic Life* (the title was altered by his literary
executor, Streatfeild). The book is a fiction
based upon Butler's own experiences supple-
mented from other sources. He cleverly dupli-
cates himself as the mature man writing the
book and as the " hero " whose life-history he is
writing. The story is told by Overton, Ernest's
godfather. This device makes it easy to tell
more about Ernest and his forbears than would
otherwise be possible with verisimilitude, for
Overton had been a playmate of Ernest's father,

---

[1] In *The Times* of February 19, 1934, was an account of a play that
would have fitted Butler's requisition. Instead of having died as in
Hamlet, the *dramatis personae* went on living, Hamlet was married, and
so on. " Ophelia reveals a limited and extremely disagreeable mind,
Polonius is as much of a bore as ever and also a drunkard, and Hamlet cannot break himself of the habit of being a tragic hero."

though he did not like him, for Theobald was
dull and mean even as a child, and of his Aunt
Alethea (based on Miss Savage), whom he liked
very much, and he remembered Ernest's parents
and grandparents and great-grandparents, and the
social environment of Ernest's youth had been
his own. He thus knew a great many things
about Ernest that Ernest himself could not know.[1]
This device enabled Butler to offer with verisimilitude a study in heredity, although, as a matter
of fact, he had a mistaken idea of his grandfather
when he wrote the sketch. (This was one of
the things he later wished to correct.) He
exposes his father, mother and sisters in a manner
that is strong meat for all but the strongest
stomachs: he exposes the wrongs done, as experienced by himself, in order that, by their
exposure, the infliction of them in the future may
be less extensive and intensive. The key to the
book is of course that " pity is a rebel passion ":
Butler was one of the sensitive who could not be
aware of suffering without doing something to
try to prevent it: he was moved by a profound
sense of injustice and a mystic belief in truth and
the right. Truth said to him, " he that loveth
father and mother, even in the form of sentiment,
more than me is not worthy of me." Butler

---

[1] Stillman, *Samuel Butler*, p. 191.

showed both the good that he approved of and
the bad that he disapproved of.

Butler's father is dealt with elsewhere in the
present book. His portrait of his mother in
The Way of All Flesh is so close that the letter
that Christina leaves for her sons to read after
her death was actually written by her; she did,
in her efforts to be " spiritually minded," refrain
from strangled fowls and blood puddings: she
was in real life given to elaborate day dreams.
That Butler's exposure of his sisters was called
for may perhaps be best established on the
testimony of Mrs. Garnett, who wrote her book,
Samuel Butler and his Family Relations, to vindicate
his family. She is telling of a time when Butler
was taken ill abroad: " the yacht of one of
Harriet's nephews by marriage was lying off the
coast. But Harriet dared not expose a young
man to the contaminating influence of the infidel.
It actually was so real a dread that she would not
allow her nephew to hear of the circumstance,
and he did not know until long afterwards that
he might have been of use." Among the other
real persons introduced into *The Way of All Flesh*
was Pauli, who appears as Towneley.

Butler came to some definite conclusions as
to the principles on which we ought to judge
other people. We must judge men not so much

by what they do as by what they make us feel
they have it in them to do. If a man has convinced you that you could trust him in an emer-
gency, he has done enough: it is what a man has
felt and aimed at that matters. Technique of
expression is of importance only as a means to
this end. How far a man has been able to express
himself to us is largely a matter of chance: " if
old Pontifex had had Cromwell's chances, he
would have done all that Cromwell did, and have
done it better." So fame is to a large extent a
matter of accident. Within the limits of accident
the man who is contemporaneously successful is
he whose capacity is a little above the average
but not too much so for the average people to
assimilate. The man who goes beyond this is
resented.

Able people seldom have able children or
grandchildren, " for the race can no more
repeat its most successful performance suddenly
than the individual can do so, and the more
brilliant the success in any one generation, the
greater as a general rule the subsequent exhaustion
until time has been allowed for recovery."

Among other Butlerian teaching in *The Way of
All Flesh* is " the duty of seeking all reasonable
pleasure and avoiding all pain that can honourably be avoided." Butler wanted people to be

happy. Butler did not advocate social reform in the ordinary sense very much, but an occasional flash of satire reveals the strength of his feeling. In this connexion in *The Way of All Flesh* is the most brilliant epigram the present writer knows— although it is only a phrase—" those virtues that make the poor respectable and the rich respected." Surely here in minimum words are contained whole volumes about convention and its effects.

The extreme subtlety of Butler's satire perplexes people sometimes. What exactly is wrong with the man described in the following passage? Is there anything culpable in anything that it says of him?

> John grew up to be a good-looking, gentlemanly fellow, with features a trifle too regular and finely-chiselled. He dressed himself so nicely, and had such good address, and stuck so steadily to his books that he became a favourite with his masters; and he had an instinct for diplomacy. John knew how to humour his father and was at a comparatively early age admitted to as much of his confidence as it was in his nature to bestow on anyone.

It may seem that Butler's inferiority complex it was merely that was functioning here. But surely it is not so. Butler felt that, as life is, the

normal man must be something of a rebel and he
who fits in too perfectly must be a tout.

There are some people who in certain relations
are generous to others but themselves do not have
generosity shown them in these relations, and
Butler was one of them.   In 1885 he met Grant
Allen and recorded a note.   It appears that when
Allen was trying to bring out his first book,
Colour Sense, it was submitted to Butler by Trübner
in its sketch state and Butler did all he could
to induce Trübner to take it, which he did.
When *Evolution Old and New* came out, Allen
reviewed it.   He laughed and sneered at it as
" leaving the reader without a single clear idea
upon any subject whatever."   When Butler met
Allen, the latter praised *Evolution Old and New* very
warmly, saying of what great use he had found it.
Butler remarks, " which indeed is true, for it has
appeared clearly enough in his books."   Later
in the year Butler wrote, " Grant Allen has
brought out his *Darwin*, and has made a handsome
acknowledgment of *Evolution Old and New* in his
preface."   He was asked to review Allen's book
but declined on the ground that " there was too
strong a personal hostility between myself and
both Darwin and Grant Allen to make it possible for
me to review the book without a bias against it."

In 1886 Butler entered as a candidate for the Slade Professorship of Fine Art at Cambridge in the vacancy created by the resignation of Sidney Colvin. He had good support but was not appointed.

In this year he casually picked up Canon Ainger's book on Charles Lamb and in it read Lamb's translation of parts of the Odyssey. He was so much attracted back to the Odyssey as to think of composing an oratorio on the subject and it was in this way that he was led to his study of the Odyssey.

"LUCK OR CUNNING AS THE MAIN MEANS OF ORGANIC MODIFICATION?"

was published in this year. It is an immensely able and vigorous book on the main issue in the theory of evolution. It is supplementary to *Life and Habit*, *Evolution Old and New*, and *Unconscious Memory*.

As usual, Butler's philosophizing, extending to things in general, keeps breaking through. Here, for example, is an attempt to formulate one aspect of the aim of life: " getting to know one's own mind more and more fully upon a greater and greater variety of subjects." Butler had the mystical faith that the inherent rightness of divine reason must prevail. He would have agreed with the maxim that you may fool all the people some of the time and some of the people all the time, but not all the people all the time.   But with him this was a mystical faith:

> I know that there is a power before which even academicism must bow, and to this power I look not unhopefully for support.

His shrewdness in observing the psychology of convention is exemplified in this utterance— " It seems as though it matters less what a man says than the number of times he repeats it in a more or less varied form." But as against this susceptibility,

> The ideal scientist should know neither self nor friend nor foe—he should be able to hobnob with those whom he most vehemently attacks, and to fly at the scientific throat of those to whom he is personally most attached; he should be neither grateful for a favourable review nor displeased at a hostile one.

Humour is as usual used to make a point, as in his reference to a man who, when he " made stepping-stones of his dead selves, jumped on them to some tune." Similarly Butler clinches the argument in favour of Lamarckism and against natural selection as explaining evolution, thus:

> Do animals and plants grow into conformity

with their surroundings because they and their
fathers and mothers take pains, or because their
uncles and aunts go away?

Surely a brilliant condensation in a humorous
sentence of one of the most important scientific
issues. Butler's courage in " standing up to "
the overpowering scientific convention of his
time deserves monumental recognition.

Grant Allen wrote a very hostile review of
Luck or Cunning? (he himself was attacked in
the book by name).

In this year, 1886, when Butler was fifty, his
father died. Among other things, this meant
that Butler was now comfortably off. He paid
off all that he had borrowed. He relieved Jones
from his pursuit of the law as a profession by
allowing him his then salary, £200 a year. In
the notebook which Butler was writing in up to
the last he wrote, " My old servant Robert had
died in August, 1886, aged seventy, and I was
too poor to get a substitute. But when my
father died at the end of December, 1886, times
were changed and I wanted someone whom I
could trust, who should be half clerk with
accountant, half private secretary, and also
generally useful." He engaged such an one,

Alfred Cathie, to his supreme satisfaction. The only other changes he made in his way of living are represented by the purchase of a new wash-basin and a new pair of hairbrushes.

After his father's death there was an immense sense of relief and revitalization, the flowering of emotional capacities which express themselves satisfyingly in varying degree and kind. Every new emotional interest that he developed now was satisfying in its measure and nature.[1]

NOTEBOOKS

Butler's second MS. volume of notes was completed by April, 1887. Here is a note in which he dealt with the assertion that the majority are always wrong: " People are generally wrong so long as a subject is new to them; but by far the greater number of things about which we are conversant are not new, and about these the majority is much the safest guide we can follow." It is perhaps worth remarking that here Butler was speaking of *really* old habits that have stood the test of real experience.

Butler was of the opinion that he was a late developer. Perhaps he exaggerated this, unless he was thinking of his productivity, but in any case he noted, " I have not developed into much,

[1] Stillman, *Samuel Butler*, p. 293.

but I have developed into much more than as a young or middle-aged man I seemed likely to do." And then he observed, as others have done, that what survives is but a fragment of a fragment: "they say that only about 10 per cent. of the heat in coal is not wasted; so with the energies even of the most able and industrious men."

In 1883 he recorded of Heatherley's having read *The Way of All Flesh*, "Mr. Heatherley said I had taken all the tenderest feelings of our nature and, having spread them carefully over the floor, stamped upon them till I had reduced them to an indistinguishable mass of filth, and then handed them round for inspection. I do not take this view of the matter myself."[1]

Butler had long got over the naïve illusion that words are exact means of representation. On the contrary, he notes, that on many subjects they are like trying to paint a miniature with a mop.

Here are some notes on biology:

The ease and breadth with which an habitual action is performed is, on a small scale, what

---

[1] That others have agreed with him is evidenced by a recent review of *The Way of All Flesh*, when it appeared in the "Everyman" series, in a religious journal : "Butler described in the greatest detail conceivable the miserable and contemptible minds and characters of his own father and mother. The result is one of the greatest novels that have ever been written. So that *The Way of All Flesh* is a liberal education."—*Scots Observer*, July 8, 1933.

the epitomizing of the life history of the race
during the embryonic stages of the individual
is on a large one.

In this last case not only are the events of
millions of years compressed into a few weeks,
but long episodes get knocked out altogether,
and results are produced not so much by a
rapid use of the appropriate means as by a
mere mental allusion to them, after which the
means seem to be dispensed with entirely, and
the effect which once required means is now
produced on the mere strength of their having
been applied formerly. We go from difficulty
with much means to facility with little means,
and finally dispense with means and whole
processes altogether.

An organ is at once the outward and visible
sign that certain wants exist, and the means of
getting them satisfied. The organ never wants
this, and will keep creating more and more
wants so that it may itself be called more and
more into existence.

Here Butler's candour gives the revelation that was
to come out of psycho-analysis, especially that
of Groddeck—the recognition of the fact that
there is an " it " that moulds our bodies and
minds independent of, and sometimes in opposi-
tion to, our conscious wills, which was no doubt

recognized by older biologists who wrote of the
flesh warring against the spirit.

In 1885 Butler says that the following epigram
is going about apropos of Mr. Gladstone's having
" kindly consented to join the Committee of the
Gordon Memorial "—

> Judas died desperate, his crime confessed;
> Had Judas flourished in our age and city,
> He'd be alive and figure with the rest
> Upon the Christ Memorial Committee.

Here are some assessments of famous composers:

> We were talking about Handel one night,
> and I said the great prevailing feeling caused
> by everything he ever wrote was " man."
> Jones agreed, and said he was first man, then
> poet, and then musician; whereas Beethoven
> was first poet, then musician, and never man
> at all.   We settled that Bach was first mechani-
> cian, then musician, then man (but not very
> much of one), and never poet at all.   Mendels-
> sohn was first hairdresser, then poetaster,
> and then musician; or, first hairdresser, then
> musician, and then poetaster.

And one of Paul:

> St. Paul said that if he had not charity he was
> as sounding brass and tinkling cymbals.   I am
> afraid it must be allowed that sometimes he had
> not charity.

One of the best criteria for finding out ultimately the rightness of a man is to find out what he believed as to the importance of his relation to the truth.   Here is a note by Butler on this point:

> I do not greatly care whether I have been right or wrong on any point, but I care a good deal about knowing which of the two I have been.

Does not this imply that what he really cared about was knowing the truth, not whether he had been right or wrong in the past? This view is supported by another note that follows at a short interval: " I care about truth not for truth's sake but for my own."   At first this view appears to be selfish, but on reflection it will be seen that it amounts to this: Past mistakes do not matter; the question is, how do you stand to the truth now? and truth does not need you, but you need the truth.

" What is the difference between a real half-crown and an imagined one? " This question has perplexed students of metaphysical idealism. Butler answered it in a note to this effect: The imagined half-crown is, as against the world, a sort of parthenogenesis. The real half-crown is strong in the vibrations of the world of men and women. In each case the imagination of the

K

individual has to be fecundated by the vibrations of the world: the vibrations of the world do not make a half-crown except with the co-operation of the imagination of the individual.

Here is a note of fundamental importance in art:

> It is not so much that you must put down what you see, as that you must put down what will convey what you have seen, and thus remind people of what they have seen themselves.

So, in acting, for example, it is not enough to act a part as you feel it: you must know and use the conventions that will convey the feelings to others. And the technique must not be obtrusive: this is the art of concealing art: " the best music should be played as the best men and women should be dressed—neither so well nor so ill as to attract attention from itself."

In the *Pall Mall Gazette* for May 31, 1887, appeared an unsigned review of *Luck or Cunning?* which was written by Mr. Bernard Shaw. The copy in the Butler collection at St. John's College, Cambridge, was given to Mr. Festing Jones by Mr. Dan Rider, who told him that Shaw's original manuscript, which he wrote on his own initiative, was very much more laudatory and much longer, but the Editor of the *Pall Mall Gazette* cut it down and took out some of the praise for fear of offending the Darwins and their friends. The article is entitled "Darwin Denounced." It militates against idolatry of men, states the issue between Darwin and Butler, and concludes:

Let it suffice to acknowledge his skilful terseness and exactness of expression, his frank disdain of affected suavity or imperturbability, his apparently but not really paradoxical humour, his racy epigrams and the geniality of his protest against "a purely automatic conception of the universe as of something that will work if a penny be dropped into the box." Ordinarily, a man who should write a book to complain that works of his had been overlooked, slighted or borrowed from without acknowledgment, would be coughed down, or even, when he went on to denounce Darwin as mean and Goethe as a writer of "dull, diseased trash" (*Wilhelm Meister*), hooted down. The fact that Mr. Butler has succeeded in doing this, and yet securing, not only a hearing, but considerable attention and interest, is a conclusive proof of the exceptional ability with which he has stated his case.

There is a letter extant from the year 1887 in which Butler stated how he stood in relation to ultimates:

Do you—does any man of science—believe that the present orthodox faith can descend many generations longer without modification? Do I—does any freethinker who has the ordinary feelings of an Englishman— doubt that the main idea underlying and running through the ordinary faith is substantially sound?

That there is an unseen life, an unseen kingdom, which is not of this world, and that the wisdom of this world is foolishness with God; that the life we live here is much, but, at the same time, small as compared with another larger life in which we all share, though, while here, we can know little if anything about it; that there is an omnipresent Being into whose presence none can enter and from whose presence none can escape; that the best are still unprofitable servants and that the wisest are still children— who that is in his senses can doubt these things? I want the church as much as I want freethought; but I want the church to pull her letter more up to date or else to avow more frankly that her letter is a letter only.

It is again, to me, disconcerting that, having just recorded Butler's real concern in religion one has to record something about his mistress, albeit something pleasant. About this time Butler, after having frequented her for some fifteen years without letting her know his name and address, invited her to tea at his rooms and introduced her to Jones. After that she came to tea several times.

At Varallo-Sesia, in northern Italy, there is a Sacro Monte. The Sacro Monte here is a mountain with shrines and chapels filled with scenes from the New Testament executed in frescoes and terra-cotta figures. Butler believed he had discovered in these works genius of the first rank, and found out that they had been executed by Gaudenzio Ferrari and Giovanni Tabachetti in the sixteenth–seventeenth centuries. He thought Ferrari one of the greatest of painters,[1] and for Tabachetti, Butler's admiration knew no bounds. He discovered that Tabachetti had come from Dinant in Belgium.

In 1887 Butler was given an official public banquet at Varallo-Sesia; and at it he was able to speak in fluent Italian. He now felt obliged, in response to this honour, to proceed forthwith

[1] Ferrari is recognized to-day as a great painter, and studies of him have appeared, since Butler wrote, in " Great Masters " series in England, Germany and France.

with his book on the Sacro Monte there. The book that Butler was now engaged in writing was, of course,

"EX VOTO."

In this work, besides his description of the works of art, illustrated with photographs taken by himself, Butler says some of the most important things he had to say about art and life, but as usual they are intermingled with just good observations. He insists on absolute sincerity as the most important thing in art (as in life). But he also holds that " realism is touching and grateful to posterity because it is turned into idealism through the impress of that seal which it is time's glory to set upon ancient things. . . . We know very well that, laugh at it as we may, our costume will three hundred years hence be as interesting as that of any other age." The best artist is at his best when his art has not yet " arrived." On either side fall the artists who are immature and those who are over-ripe.[1] Among his great artists are Homer and Shakespeare at their best, the artists of the Venus de Milo and the Ilyssus, the artists of the finest work of Rembrandt, Giorgione and Velasquez, and Handel and Tabachetti.

[1] In *The Times Literary Supplement* for November 17, 1932, was written: " The moment a style in furniture reaches perfection, its soundness of construction and use of materials decline."

It is only after generations of imposture that approximate right gets done. True, Guido, Guercino and Domenichino have at last tumbled into the abyss, but they had a triumph of some three hundred years, during which none dared lift hand against them.

Though tens of thousands of men and women of genius are as dandelion seeds borne upon the air and perishing without visible result, yet there is here and there a seed that really does take root.

Here is Butler's view as to how to learn to become an artist—given, of course, the ability—

The only way to study an art is to begin at once with doing something that one wants very badly to do, and doing it—even though it be only very badly. Study, of course, but synchronously—letting the work be its own exercises. . . . Jones, talking with me on this subject, said, "Oh, that men should put an enemy in their brains to steal away their hearts!"

Butler's quite extraordinary insight is illustrated in the following passage :

That the letter of the coming faith will be greatly truer than that of the many that have preceded it, I for one do not believe. Let us have no more "Lo heres" and "Lo theres" in this respect. I would as soon have a winking Madonna or a forged decretal as the doubtful experiments or garbled articles which the high priests of modern science are applauded with one voice for trying to palm off on their devotees; and I should look as hopefully for good result from a new monastery as from a new school of art, college of music or scientific institution. Whatever faith or science the world bows down to will in its letter be tainted with the world that worships it. Whoever clings to the spirit that underlies all science obtaining among civilized peoples will assuredly find that he cannot serve God and Mammon. The true Christ ever brings a sword on earth as well as peace, and if he maketh men to be of one mind in a house, he divideth a house no less surely. The way will be strait in the future as in the past. All that can be hoped for is that it may perhaps become a trifle more easy through the work of just men made perfect through suffering that have gone before, and that he who in bygone ages would have been burnt will now only be scouted.

Perhaps the most important passage in the book, as expressing Butler on ultimates, is:

That there is a Holy Spirit and that it does

descend on those that diligently seek it, who
can for a moment question? Who that need
be reckoned with denies the eternal underlying
verity that there is an omnipresent unknown
something for which Mind, Spirit, or God is,
as Professor Mivart has well said, "the least
misleading" expression?

These are the most important passages in *Ex
Voto*, but incidentally Butler has some good
remarks on the art of acting. "The physical
conditions of the stage involve compliance with
conventions from which there is no escape."
Actors, he says (writing in 1888, be it remembered), should subordinate themselves to the
unity of design in the play: not crowd each other
out because of being "stars." One criterion of
goodness in acting is so to act as to give the
requisite subordination of the character concerned. On the other hand, "we can spare a
good deal of Hamlet; but if the part is totally
excised—even though the Hamlet be Mr. Irving
himself—the play must suffer." This last is a
very typical Butlerism—really carefully thought
out, carefully studied in expression, but passed
off as it might be a slip.

The book was published in 1888 under the
title, *Ex Voto : An Account of the Sacro Monte or
New Jerusalem at Varallo-Sesia*. This was the

last of Butler's publications to bear the imprint
" Op. —."

After the publication of *Ex Voto* Butler sent
to Dinant and discovered that Tabachetti's real
name was Jean de Wespin, but that, like several
members of his family, he was known as Tabaquet
and by the Italianized form Tabachetti.

In 1888 also, *Narcissus*, the mock-heroic
oratorio by Butler and Jones, was published.
Mr. Fuller Maitland, the music critic of *The
Times*, had such a high opinion of this work that
he wrote that the " majestic choruses " were
" worthy of Handel at his best."

A journal called *The Universal Review* was
started in this year, edited by a certain Harry
Quilter, who knew Butler slightly and asked him
to write an article for it. He wrote " Quis
desiderio . . . ," surely one of the funniest and at
the same time best-written articles that one can
call to mind. Butler wrote further articles for
this journal.

In this year, 1888, Butler was asked by the
leading members of the Shrewsbury Archaeo-
logical Society to write a short memoir of his
grandfather for their Quarterly Journal. His
sisters gave him his grandfather's correspondence
from 1790 to 1839, and it was to Butler a revela-

tion. He fell in love with his grandfather and set to work to write a full-dress biography.

About the year 1888 Butler wrote a paper, " On Knowing what gives us Pleasure." In it he tells that in America he was shown over a private art collection by the owner, who " knew what he liked." Butler found the following formula to deal with the situation, when he was called upon to give his verdict, " This collection would vie with any similar one in the old country, or indeed in any part of the world."

In 1889 appeared in *The Universal Review* an article by Butler entitled " The Aunt, the Nieces and the Dog." It was mostly taken up with actual letters of an almost illiterate person which had come into his hands through Jones and which reveal real-life comedy for which Butler had a flair. But in the article are also some of Butler's typical philosophical observations:

When a thing is old, broken and useless, we throw it on the dust-heap, but when it is sufficiently old, sufficiently broken and sufficiently useless, we give money for it, put it into a museum, and read papers over it, which people come long distances to hear.

So when people are in a bad way, we neglect

them, but if they are on the point of death, we place every resource our hospitals can command at their disposal and show no stint in our consideration for them.   We are generous if we do not fear.

Little things gall us out of proportion—that one should have said this or that little unkind or wanton saying; that he should have gone away from this or that hotel and given a shilling too little to the waiter.

The man who insists on seeing things for himself and uttering what he finds will suffer.

Another article in *The Universal Review* in the same year was " A Medieval Girl School." This again is predominantly humorous, describing a medieval painting, but again has its serious passages. Butler argues for Christianity not being interpreted as asceticism.

The essence of Christianity lies in faith in an unseen world, in doing one's duty, in speaking the truth, in finding the true life rather in others than in oneself, and in the certain hope that he who loses his life on these behalfs finds more than he has lost.   What can agnosticism do against such Christianity as this ?

If we could see either great branch of the Church make a frank, authoritative attempt to bring its teaching into greater harmony with

the educated understanding and conscience of
the time, then I, for one, in view of the difficulty and graciousness of the task, and in view
of the great importance of historical continuity,
would gladly sink much of my own private
opinion and would gratefully help either
Church or both. Can the leaders of the Church
be blind to the restlessness of the current that
has set against those literal interpretations? . . .
The clergyman is wanted as supplementing
the doctor and the lawyer in all civilized
communities.

Butler completed his third MS. volume of
notes by 1890. Here are two of the notes, first
one on Christianity:

Christianity was only a very strong and
singularly well-timed Salvation Army movement that happened to receive help from an
unusual and highly dramatic incident. It was
a Puritan reaction in an age when, no doubt, a
Puritan reaction was much wanted; but like
all sudden violent reactions, it soon wanted
reacting against.

The second note from volume III I wish to
quote is about his experience of the public:

I have not found the public generous, but
what public ever was or can be generous? I

have found the public suspicious, supercilious, quick to carp, slow to praise, and bent on driving as hard a bargain with me as it could; but why should I find it anything else? Do I care much about the public, *qua* people whom I do not know personally, or try to tickle it? Hardly. If, then, I say what I choose to say without thinking of the public, why should I grumble at the public for not thinking of me?

Besides, not being paid myself, I can in better conscience use the works of others, as I daily do, without paying for them, and without being at the trouble of praising or thanking them more than I have a mind to.

Nevertheless, the English public is not generous. The Gladstone ministry might leave Gordon in the lurch as long as they pleased and they stood in no danger of being turned out, but when our beer was touched we upset the ministry immediately.

In 1890 Butler published in *The Universal Review* three articles on " The Deadlock in Darwinism." They are masterly and afford the best summary of Butler's scientific philosophy in his own words that there is, and, incidentally, contain his reply to Weismann. His philosophical

observation comes out in such a passage as the
following:

> Love of self-display, and the want of single-
> ness of mind that it inevitably engenders—
> these, I suppose, are the sins that glaze the
> casements of most men's minds; and from
> these, no matter how hard he tries to free him-
> self, nor how much he despises them, who is
> altogether exempt?

In the same year and in the same journal Butler
published "Ramblings in Cheapside," a title
which covers deep thought rendered assimilable
by humour and lightness of touch. Butler recognized that, as regards our apprehension of reality,
"Our utmost seeing is but a fumbling of blind
finger-ends in an overcrowded pocket." He
satirizes convention and the hold it has on public
opinion, but recognizes that there is a residuum
of mulishness in it, in which, for some, there is
hope. For the most part, however, those who
control public opinion must hear and see their
own names and the right words repeated often
enough. Seldom does a really good man come
to his own in his own generation. The public
"have staked their money on the wrong man so
often without suspecting it that when there comes
one whom they suspect, it would be madness not
to bet against him." Butler, again, expresses the

doctrine, " Everyone is an immortal to himself, for he cannot know that he is dead until he is dead, and when dead, how can he know anything about anything? "

The Universal Review ceased publication in December, 1890. In the two-and-a-half years of its existence, ten articles by Butler had appeared in it.

In pursuing the theme of the Odyssey for an oratorio, Butler read the poem in Greek and was fascinated by a mystery he felt in it. He proceeded to translate it—" with the same benevolent leaning (say) towards Tottenham Court Road that Messrs. Butcher and Lang have shown towards Wardour Street." In other words, Butler believed that the Odyssey was originally written in the language of its own time and place, i.e., it had the quality of contemporaneousness. If, therefore, we are to have the Odyssey in English, it ought to have the quality of contemporaneousness. It is generally admitted that the classical age of translation into English was the sixteenth century, and that is precisely the time when translators translated into the language of their own age. I have heard a distinguished classical scholar, the late Professor Phillimore, say that Butcher and Lang is English of no date.

Butler's thoroughness was such that in translating
the Odyssey (and, later, the Iliad), he learnt
nearly the whole by heart, although he found, to
his chagrin, that he could retain only a few books
at a time. While studying the Odyssey, Butler
suddenly got the notion that the author was a
young woman. The more he thought about it,
the more it seemed to him that this was the
solution of the difficulties that had eluded him.

Writing to a friend, a lady, in 1891, he said:

Ulysses is getting on. He is in the castle
now, and Penelope wanted him to have his feet
washed and he said he would rather not. He
was not going to let any of these " cats " (it
was not " cats " but " Mrs Dogs," only that
will not be fit for publication) wash his feet;
but Penelope insisted that washed he certainly
must be, once that night, and then again to-
morrow morning; so it was settled that
Euryclea was to wash him, and she got some
cold water and poured it into a bath, then she
added the hot until it was just right, and then
she began to scrub. By and by she found the
scar, and this surprised her so much that she
dropped the foot into the water with a splash,
and it upset the tub, so that Euryclea had to
go and fetch some more water, for the first was
all spilt; but he did get washed in the end.

You may think this exaggerated, but see
Butcher and Lang, Book XIX, about two
thirds through, and you will find every word
of it.

Evolution was the subject of a letter which
Professor Marcus Hartog wrote to Butler at this
time, and in his reply Butler wrote of the
biologists as follows:

They were driven into Weismann much as
sailors are driven to port in a storm, and even
if he will not shelter them, there is nothing but
their skill in hoodwinking the public which
will save them from disaster. Fortunately for
them, the public has developed such hereditary
aptitude for being cheated, and they have
developed such not less hereditary aptitude for
gulling the public that, thanks to the universities and the academies, they will probably find
enough supporters to last their time, after
which the deluge will not much matter.

It can hardly be denied that the orthodoxy of
Weismannism has very considerably weakened.

In 1892, while working on the Odyssey, Butler
" came to Neptune's turning the Phaeacian ship
into a rock at the entrance to the harbour of

Scheria, and felt sure that, if an actual place was being described anywhere in the poem, this was the passage or one of the passages. He made a list of the various natural features of Scheria, as detailed in the poem," and proceeded to look on the map for where they could be satisfied. Learning from Colonel Mure's *Language and Literature of Ancient Greece* that the locality of the episode of the Cyclopes had been supposed to be near the Lilyboean promontory, he got hold of the Admiralty charts of the neighbourhood, whereon he found that Trapani and Mount Eryx in Sicily supplied everything he was in search of. He then wrote to *The Athenaeum* about it. On the day that his letter appeared, he gave his lecture at the Working Men's College in Great Ormond Street on " The Humour of Homer." Shortly after, another letter by him in *The Athenaeum* argued that the description of Ithaca does not agree with the island called Ithaca, and that the Odyssean Ithaca, when it is being described from within, is drawn from Trapani and its neighbourhood.

In 1892 Butler's mistress died—at the age of forty-one, from consumption. Butler saw to it that she was properly buried: such is the irony of human weakness.

Butler had worked out his thesis of the authoress of the Odyssey to the details that she was hardly more than seventeen or eighteen and that she wrote before 1000 B.C. He wrote a lecture which he entitled " Was the Odyssey written by a woman? " which he delivered to two or three small societies in 1893. His attention having for long been turned to unconscious humour, he worked into this lecture some illustrations of this phenomenon from the Book of Common Prayer:

> Give peace in our time, O Lord, because there is none other that fighteth for us but only thou, O God.

> Almighty and everlasting God, who alone workest great marvels, send down upon our Bishops and Curates and all Congregations committed to their charge the healthful spirit of thy grace.

On April 24, 1893, the West Central group of the Fabian Society in London had Butler to deliver this lecture to it. The meeting was a tiny one held in the rooms of the late Graham Wallas at 32 Great Ormond Street.[1] The following account of the group has been given by Mr. Bernard Shaw:

[1] For the date, the finding of which took much trouble, and the place I am obliged to Mr. F. W. Galton, Secretary of the Fabian Society.

It consisted of two or three members who used to discuss bi-metallism. I was a member geographically, but never attended. One day I saw on the notice of meetings which I received an announcement that Samuel Butler would address the group on the authorship of the Odyssey. Knowing that the group would have no notion of how great a man they were entertaining, I dashed down to the meeting, took the chair, and gave the audience (about five strong including Butler and myself) to understand that the occasion was a great one. According to the narrative of Festing Jones—at the close of the lecture, Shaw said that when he had heard of the title first, he supposed that it was some mere fad or fancy of Butler's, but that, on turning up the Odyssey to see what could have induced him to take it up, he had not read a hundred lines before he found himself saying, " Why, of course it is a woman." And he spoke so strongly that people who had only laughed all through the lecture began to think that there might be something in it after all.[1] Shaw's narrative continues:

Considering how extraordinary a man Butler is now seen to have been, there is something

---

[1] Shaw is the " well-known and very able writer " referred to by Butler in *The Authoress of the Odyssey*, p. 208.

tragic in the fact that the greatest genius
among the long list of respectable dullards who
have addressed us never got beyond this
absurd little group.[1]

In a letter in 1893, writing about being converted
to an opinion, Butler expressed himself as follows:

You may be quite sure that if I did agree
with you, I should at once come round to your
opinion, for all I care about is to be on the
winning side, and I should at once go over to
the one that I thought the strongest.

Butler completed the fourth MS. volume of
his notes by 1893, and the only note I will
quote from this volume is appropriate:

A little levity will save many a good heavy
thing from sinking.

He now turned to translating the Iliad. Here
is a specimen passage chosen by himself in 1894:

As the flakes that fall thick upon a winter's
day, when Jove is minded to snow and to
display these his arrows to mankind—he lulls
the wind to rest and snows steadily till he has
covered the tops of the high mountains, the
headlands that jut out into the sea, the grassy
plains and the tilled fields of man; the snow

[1] In Pease, *History of the Fabian Society*, p. 105.

falls on the forelands and havens of the grey sea, but the wandering wave resists it, though all things else are wrapped as with a mantle, so heavy are the heavens with snow.

Jones had introduced to Butler a young Swiss named Faesch, who became very intimate with them. On his leaving for Switzerland, Butler wrote a poem of farewell to him which is remarkable for its revelation of depth of feeling and its religious language. Faesch was puzzled by the latter, but Butler replied: " I know no words that express a deeply felt hope so well as those I have used, and the fact that others make money by prostituting them shall not stop me from using them when I am in the humour for doing so." It is very remarkable how Butler's parental love gushed out on Faesch. In a letter to Faesch he wrote pathetically of a dog making a fuss of him, " I was so flattered at being made up to by anyone or anything who seemed to tell me that I was a nice person that I let him go and hunt for rats all over me."

Butler had a nice confirmation of his Odyssey theory at this time. In the poem Ulysses, sailing from Calypso's island (Pantellaria), " steered towards the Great Bear, which is also called the Wain, keeping it on his left hand, for

so Calypso advised him." Butler wrote to
Greenwich asking for direction on this point.
The Astronomer Royal replied that if Ulysses had
started from Pantellaria about 3000 years ago
(Butler dated the Odyssey not later than 1100 or
1050 B.C. or earlier than 1150 or 1200 B.C.) and
followed Calypso's sailing orders, he would have
arrived at Trepani.

In some autobiographical notes written in 1896
Butler said:

There can be little doubt that it was the
publication of *Evolution Old and New* that led
Mr. Darwin in the following November to
publish his *Erasmus Darwin*, a book which
brought about a very bitter controversy between Mr. Darwin and myself, in which I had
the whole of the academic and scientific world,
without, so far as I know, a single exception,
against me. I had no support from a single
academic or scientific quarter, while the abuse
that was heaped upon me was more un-
measured than I have had to encounter at any
other period of my career. . . . I have seen the
theory I advanced in *Life and Habit* taken as a
matter of course by the man who was the most
angry in his attacks on me—the late Mr. G. J.
Romanes.

Butler experienced the mulishness of the orthodox. He wrote, " The more they see us anxious to get them to think as we do, the more they will stick to their own opinion. It piques them far more and makes them far more uneasy if we make them see that we do not care one straw how they think." It is not surprising in this connexion to find a note of Butler's in this year that he had often thought of writing an *Erewhon Revisited*.

His *Life* of his grandfather was published in this year.

" LIFE AND LETTERS OF SAMUEL BUTLER."

Butler records of his grandfather that, when he was a boy, he gave most of his time to pursuits other than book learning, and yet he could do his lessons almost instantaneously and with the greatest success.

The biography is full of people and the life of the times with which it deals. One person of outstanding ability in its record is Baron Merian, Russian Plenipotentiary at Paris. Here are some of the things from his letters:

Your countrymen, all blazing with everlasting glory, are too apt to overlook ninety-nine good things because, forsooth, the hundredth is wanting! Just as if they had never heard of the great maxim " Que le mieux est l'ennemi du bien."

Johnson did not know what a rake is, and had recourse to the *Edda* instead of asking his farmer.

There is another doctification in the notes to *Coriolanus* about " quarry." Why, " quarry " is nothing in the world but *curée*.

In a letter to Dr. Butler, the Duke of Sussex wrote, in 1829:

The game is not easy to play; for we must oppose calmness and reason to violence and misrepresentation; but as the former economize strength and the latter waste it, so we must tire out our antagonists.

Butler in the conclusion to the *Life* wrote as follows:

He who shrinks from expressing an opinion which may be reasonably asked will ere long shrink from forming one that he should reasonably form. Nothing induces to indolence and timidity of thought like indolence and timidity of expression. Expression is to the mind what action is to the bodily organ, and he who would be vigorous in thought must be prompt and fearless in expression also.

In a letter in 1897 he emphasized this, saying,

" When people make omelettes they must break eggs."

Butler's portrait was painted by his friend Gogin in 1896. It is now in the National Portrait Gallery. It is most remarkable for the sense it conveys, especially through the eyes, of *penetrating power*—a feature that people who knew Butler commented on frequently.

Butler now wrote

" THE AUTHORESS OF THE ODYSSEY."

He believed it to be much the most important thing he had done. When objection was taken to its unacademic manner, he wrote, " I considered that if I stated my case in the academic manner I should not move the academic people and I should lose the ordinary club and cultured women readers who in the long run force the academic people to follow them."

The subject of the book has been dealt with above. Incidental passages, however, have intrinsic interest, as, for example, the observation that " in both the *Iliad* and the *Odyssey* the status of women is represented as being much what it is at present, and as incomparably higher than it was in the Athenian civilization with which we are best acquainted."

Incidentally, too, he develops his criticism of
the academic:

> Men of science, so far as I have observed
> them, are apt in their fear of jumping to a con-
> clusion to forget that there is such a thing as
> jumping away from one.

He says that there is danger to our great educational establishments in their " letting dead mind
remain unconsumed in their system."

> Since, do what we will, we can no more
> detect the one genius who may be born among
> a multitude of good average children than
> Herod could detect the King of the Jews among
> the babes of Bethlehem, we have no course but
> to do as Herod did, and lay violent hands upon
> all young people until we have reduced every
> single one of them to such mediocrity as may
> be trusted to take itself off sooner or later.   To
> this end we have established schools and
> schoolmen; nor is it easy to see how we could
> more effectively foster that self-sufficiency
> which does so much towards helping us
> through the world, and yet repress any
> exuberance of originality or independence
> of thought which might be prejudicial to
> its possessor during his own life, and
> burdensome to posterity when he is dead and
> gone.

Obviously wise, however, and necessary as our present system is, we nevertheless grumble at it. We would have any number of first-class geniuses in art, literature and music, and yet have plenty of elbow-room for ourselves. Our children too; they cannot show too many signs of genius, but at the same time we blame them if they do not get on in the world and make money as genius next to never does. We would have others forgotten, and yet not be forgotten ourselves.

What has the erudition of the last 2,000 years done for the Iliad and the Odyssey but to emend the letter in small things and obscure the spirit in great ones?

A band of scholars a century or two before the birth of Christ refused to see the Iliad and the Odyssey as the work of the same person, but erudition snubbed them and snuffed them out so effectively that for some 2,000 years they were held to have been finally refuted. Can there be a more scathing satire on the value of scholastic criticism? It seems as though Minerva had shed the same darkness over both the poems that she shed over Ulysses, that they might go in and out among eminent scholars from generation to generation and none should see them.

Butler dwells on the extraordinary nature of the Odyssey:

> The interest of the poem ostensibly turns mainly on the revenge taken by a bald, middle-aged gentleman, whose little remaining hair is red, on a number of young men who have been eating him out of house and home while courting his supposed widow.

Here, anon, is an epigram: "What is an appropriate quotation for if not to be appropriated?"

And, finally, here is Butler's description of the essence of art:

> What really stirs us is the communion of the still living mind of the man or woman to whom we owe it, and the conviction that that mind is as we would have our own to be.

Butler's argument that the author of the Odyssey was a woman is by no means so far-fetched as it sounds. Bentley said that the Iliad was written for men and the Odyssey for women. Butler in his schooldays used to say that the Odyssey was the Iliad's wife and that it was written by a clergyman. Colonel Mure pointed out that in Phaeacia "the women engross the chief parts of the small stock of common sense allotted to the community." Butler in his book was able to argue the staggering ignorance of the most ordinary matters in the life of a man, the authoress's sly digs at her father, her understanding of her mother, and so on.

" In the *Authoress of the Odyssey*," wrote Mrs. Stillman, " whether she was actually the authoress or not, Butler portrayed with inner truth a real woman, and he who had never seen anything from a woman's point of view and who had never cared much for women or taken seriously their efforts to become individuals, had now with loving care and sympathy entered into the soul of a young, high-spirited girl, gifted, affectionate, emotionally undeveloped, deeply feminine and ardently feministic. It is one of the major miracles of his career."[1]

Those who were convinced by Butler included Lord Grimthorpe, Justice Wills, Bernard Shaw, Robert Bridges and Mandell Creighton. In 1929 was published *Samuel Butler and the Odyssey* by B. Farrington, Senior Lecturer in Classics in the University of Capetown, espousing Butler's views. In it he wrote:

Diamonds roll down the river beds of Africa along with common pebbles, but the diamonds stick when they reach the prepared surface in the Kimberley works. Butler's mind was such a surface.

[1] *Samuel Butler*, p. 270.

Let us see the authoress of the Odyssey, discovered by Butler, as described by Mrs. Stillman. Nausicaa thought men coarse, foolish and tiresome. She resented the insignificance of women. She poked fun at men; she did not enter into their point of view and she did not want to; but she wrought with loving attention to show the women wise, clever, industrious, influential, or, if they lacked any of these qualities, to whitewash them if possible, to punish them if not. Women beguile Ulysses, rescue him, wait for him, recognize him, manage him. The authoress is very much alive to the tragedies of women: she hardly recognizes that men have any. Throughout the poem Butler felt " an exquisite sense of weakness." Butler liked Nausicaa for being exquisitely feminine and utterly unfemale.[1]

In 1897 Pauli caught a cold and had to take to bed. " At Boulogne, Butler received one communication from the nurse and then for three days nothing. He returned to London and next day read in *The Times* that Pauli had died on December 29, exactly eleven years, to the day, after the death of Canon Butler. Butler was communicated with by the undertaker and went to the funeral. The party travelled by train

[1] Stillman, *Samuel Butler*, pp. 281–2.

and in conversation in the train with other
'mourners' he asked where Pauli had lived.
He was told that he had lived in Belgrave Man-
sions, Grosvenor Gardens, S.W." It seemed
that the rooms were very cheap, only £120 a year,
which was less than he had paid before when
living in Bruton Street. (Butler was paying
£28 rent for his rooms, about £36 including
rates and taxes.) Then Butler asked, "Have you
any idea how much Pauli made by his profession?" One of his fellow-travellers replied,
"I do not know how he has been doing of late
years, but many years ago—perhaps twenty, but
I cannot be certain—he told me he was earning
about £700." Butler remembered his father
having written to him in 1879 that he had been
told that Pauli was making £1,000 a year, and
how Pauli had indignantly denied that he was
making more than his bare expenses. Then it
appeared that Pauli had left his brother £1,000,
"as though," wrote Butler later, "there were
more than £1,000 disposed of under Pauli's
will. And here the reserve which I had maintained very sufficiently broke down. I had been
shocked at learning the style in which Pauli
evidently lived, and the amount he had been
making at the Bar while doing his utmost to
convince me that he was not clearing anything at

all." He learnt subsequently from Pauli's solicitor that Pauli's greatest receipts from his practice in any one year were from £800 to £900, but that during the last few years he had done less, owing to his frequent illnesses and had not taken more than about £500 or £600. Pauli had been contributed to by another friend, Charles Swinburne. The latter knew nothing of Butler's relations with Pauli any more than Butler knew about Swinburne's. There was another man too. The net value of Pauli's estate was about £9,000. He left Butler nothing. In talking with Pauli's solicitor Butler said, " Well, after all, he has as good as left me £200 a year—not to mention the lunches."

In the *Fortnightly Review* for December, 1897, appeared an article on Shakespeare's sonnets by William Archer arguing that the patron was the Earl of Pembroke and in the number for the following February appeared an article by Sidney Lee arguing for Southampton. This reading led Butler to take up the study of the sonnets, which he did with his usual thoroughness—learning them by heart, cutting them out without numbers and rearranging them on a table, etc. He came to the conclusion that all but a very few were addressed to a young man called William Hews.

No doubt Butler's attitude to Pauli affected his
interpretation.   Much of the grossness that has
been attributed to his interpretation is quite
wrong.

In 1898 Butler revised some notes that he had
made about his father in 1887, so we know what
he thought of him as late in his life as this.   His
opinion since his books, *Erewhon*, *The Fair Haven*,
and *The Way of All Flesh*, had not altered.   In
these notes we find the following:

> My mother's last illness and death, in 1873,
> were ascribed by the whole family to my
> heartless conduct in having written *Erewhon*;
> the doctors, however, declared that she was
> suffering from cancer of the stomach.

> Uncongenial as my father and I were to one
> another, we were cordial friends as compared
> with my father and my brother.   My brother
> hated my father with a fury it would not be
> easy to surpass, and my father's feelings to my
> brother were not far removed from this.
> When I was staying at Shrewsbury a few years
> since, he said of Tom, " I don't care about
> knowing where he is, so long as we hear of his
> death."

In 1898, elsewhere, Butler wrote, " My father
repeatedly taunted me with ' living in idleness '

upon him. I was working as hard as any man
could work."

In 1898 Butler wrote a preface to the second
volume of his MS. notes, in which he said,
" They grew as, with little disturbance, they now
stand. . . . That this book will be looked over by
not a few, I doubt not."

In 1899 Butler wrote in a letter:

I never write on any subject unless I believe
the opinion of those who have the ear of the
public to be mistaken, and this involves, as a
necessary consequence, that every book I
write runs counter to the men who are in
possession of the field.

In this year Robert Bridges (whose brother
married one of Butler's sisters) wrote to Butler,
à propos *The Authoress of the Odyssey*, " There can
be no doubt that it is one of the most valuable
books on the Homeric question." Later he
wrote, " Your history of *The Fair Haven* aston-
ishes me; so few copies sold! I have a copy—
many thanks—and have almost all your books;
the only gaps being due to the over-apprecia-
tion of borrowers. I always hold you up as
one of the best stylists. You taught me a great
deal."

"EREWHON REVISITED."

About the turn of the century Butler wrote *Erewhon Revisited*. On the half-title he wrote:

Him do I hate even as I hate Hell fire,
Who says one thing, and hides another in his
    heart.   —Iliad, ix, 312, 313.

The book is a brilliant but daring satire on organized Christianity. It was written with running pen, and Butler judged it to be decidedly better than *Erewhon*.

He speaks of a man who "had earned a high reputation for sobriety of judgment by resolutely refusing to have definite views on any subject." Anon he paints a picture of an old church:

How peaceful it was, with its drowsy, old-world smell of ancestor, dry rot, and stale incense. As the clouds came and went, the grey-green, cobweb-chastened light ebbed and flowed over the walls and ceiling; to watch the fitfulness of its streams was a sufficient occupation. A hen laid an egg outside and began to cackle—it was an event of magnitude; a peasant sharpening his scythe, a blacksmith hammering at his anvil, the clack of a wooden shoe upon the pavement. . . .

Here are some utterances of his ultimate beliefs:

Faith consists in holding that the intuitions of the best men and women are in themselves an evidence which may not be set aside lightly.

Good is gold; it is rare, but it will not tarnish. Evil is like dirty water—plentiful and foul, but it will run itself clear of taint.

Our sense of moral guilt varies inversely as the squares of its distance in time and space from ourselves.

We approach Him most nearly when we think of Him as our expression for Man's highest conception of goodness, wisdom and power. But we cannot rise to him above the level of our own highest selves.

Here is a passage with the lash of satire, concerning " Bridgeford ":

The readiness of her Professors to learn from those who at first sight may seem least able to instruct them—the gentleness with which they correct an opponent if they feel it incumbent upon them to do so, the promptitude with which they acknowledge an error when it is pointed out to them, and quit a position, no matter how deeply they have been committed to it, at the first moment at which they see that they cannot hold it righteously, their delicate sense of humour, their utter immunity from what the Sunchild used to call log-rolling or intrigue, the scorn with which they regard anything like hitting below the belt. . . .

Finally, we have as a general comment on the message of the true prophet:

" These are hard sayings," said Dr. Downie. " I know they are," replied my father, " and I do not like saying them, but there is no royal road to unlearning, and you have much to unlearn. . . .

" The masses distrust the church and are on their guard against aggression, whereas they do not suspect the doctrinaires and faddists, who, if they could, would interfere in every concern of our lives."

" You want a heart to check your head and a head to check your heart."

In his satire Butler regularly drew upon real life—some persons and practices cannot be satirized, they have only to be seen aright and the criticism of them is evident. So in *Erewhon Revisited*. For example, of one incident Butler wrote:

I forget whether I have said that all the part of Hanky's sermon dealing with the Sunchild evidence is taken almost word for word from a letter in *The Times* that appeared December 8, 1892, and was written by Sir Gabriel Stokes and

Lord Halsbury, asking for money on behalf of the Christian Evidence Society.

The advertisement in *Erewhon* of " Dedication trousers " was taken word for word from one exhibited at the time of the Thanksgiving Service at St. Paul's for the recovery of the Prince of Wales, except that " Dedication " was substituted for " Thanksgiving."

On the reviewing of books Butler wrote to a correspondent in 1900:

I have always observed that it is the shallow books that are received with a chorus of applause. The critics can understand these at once; but as for being at any pains to study what requires sustained attention—is it to be expected of them? Besides—do you review books yourself? If you do, by all means let the fact be known in literary circles. The re-viewers themselves sometimes write books and, if they know you are able to belaud them, they will belaud you; otherwise if you write on a subject of which they know nothing, if they deign to notice you at all, they will make it quite plain that they have not thought it worth while to read what you have said. The art of reading is being rapidly lost; there is nothing in journalism now but skin and a show of smartness.

In this year Butler wrote to Bridges of the latter's poems:

The residuary impression, which I had already formed by having read extracts, was fully confirmed, and we had no question that we were reading poetry of a very high order; but as regards myself, you know as well as I do that I am not a poetically minded man. I have never read and never, I am afraid, shall read a line of Keats or Shelley or Coleridge or Wordsworth except such extracts as I occasionally see in the Royal Academy catalogues. I have read *The Idylls of the King* and I do not like them. I have never read a word of Browning—save as above. There is no concealing the fact that it is the business, practical side of literature and not the poetical and imaginative —I mean literature applied to the solving of some difficult problem which may be usefully solved—that alone fires me with hot desire to devour and imitate it. That, and the battering down of falsehood to the uttermost of my poor ability.

Who can appreciate contemporary literature? It is most certain that neither you nor I can form even an approximate idea of what our respective literary positions will be fifty years after we are dead; for it would be mere affectation on the part of either of us to doubt that a position of some sort will be awarded to us—to you as a poet, to me as a prose writer. Festing Jones says that the passage in which Wordsworth is referred to is not literally true. For example, Butler came back once from his people's and said that he had found a volume of Wordsworth there and that he admired a great deal of it.

Anon Butler writes to Bridges:

I find *King Lear* and *Othello* abound with gems of the purest lustre, but I do not like either of these plays and never read them—for the horror and repulsiveness of the story. Of Keats:

If he were ever going to be more to me, some magnet would have drawn us together before now; and I assure you I am beginning to feel that my period of active work is manifestly drawing to a close.

In 1900 Jones's mother died, leaving him adequately provided for, and thereupon of course the allowance that Butler had been making him was brought to an end. Butler would not accept repayment of what he had allowed Jones, but before Butler died, Jones executed a covenant that his executors should, after his death, repay the amount to Butler or to his estate.

NOTEBOOKS AGAIN.

Butler completed volume 5 of his MS. notes in March, 1900. Here is a note on a problem that is quite unexplained by orthodox science:

It is curious that the ideas of plants concerning beauty should be so much the same as our own notwithstanding the remoteness of the connection between us. And so with butterflies and insects. The canons of form, colour, pattern, and even to some extent of sound seem to have been arrived at at an early stage of organic development.

Here is one on " femaleness " in human nature:

Every man was his mother once as well as his father, and every woman was her father as well as her mother, but the male has a longer and more intimate sojourn with his mother than the female has had with her father. Whether this in any way tends to explain the fact that more females are born than males; and whether again hermaphrodites are more often undecided males or undecided females—these are points to be considered.

Here is an interesting note on theories of multiple authorship:

The multiple origin of Homer is like the theories about Shakespeare that reach us from America. I would as soon believe that Shakespeare was written by a syndicate as that the Iliad and Odyssey are not each of them written from first to last by a single author. Can those who maintain that each of the two poems is by various writers find one single example of a long poem pieced together as they suppose the Iliad and Odyssey to have been, and yet preserving such an appearance of unity? I fully believe that each writer added to and modified his work in, so to speak, successive editions; but I can detect no change of hand. If asked to give an example of an author so modifying and enlarging his work, Piers Plowman occurs to me at once; and I do not doubt other examples could be found.

Here is a very characteristic note on his failure to achieve contemporary success:

THE VICTORIAN AGE. Naturally I consider its most discreditable feature to be the way in which I have been myself neglected; and probably most other authors who are aware that they are more or less failures look at the matter much as I do.

On the question of university education he writes:

Some few have got good (I do not mean fellowships or money) out of the universities, but these are men who would get good out of anything.

Illumination on the fact that Butler was really a prophet with a message that burned to be delivered is afforded by the following:

I trust I may see no more after I can say no more. I can fancy no death-bed more distressing than that on which a man feels the weight of an undelivered message, which he knows, and which no one else is likely to hit upon, but which he cannot deliver.

Butler's ideas of heaven and hell are interesting, especially when compared with those of Mr. Bernard Shaw:

SUBJECT. A dream of heaven in which everything is made to go a little wrong, without which there would be no happiness. Hell should consist in the utter absence of all disagreeable stimulant—only enough stimulant being allowed to prevent sleep.

The following passage is of unusual interest as showing Butler's judgment on a contemporary and how it has been endorsed, as well as criteria he went by:

MAETERLINCK. I believe, or strongly suspect
that people will not think as highly of him in
ten years as they do now. He has sat at the
feet of Plato, Marcus Aurelius, Carlyle, and
Emerson—I say nothing about Plotinus and
Novalis for I do not know them. The others
I have tried and at no such feet can I sit.
They have no message for me. Plato is the
best, his *Apology* is splendid; his descriptions of
scenery and his episodial (if there is such a
word) chats with friends on a fresh summer
morning are delightful; but, take him all
round, my feeling towards him is much what
I gather Aristophanes to have entertained, and
he is not for me.

Carlyle, again, is for me too much like
Wagner, of whom Rossini said that he has
" des beaux moments mais des mauvais quarts
d'heure "—my French is not to be trusted.
I have never read a line of Marcus Aurelius
that leaves me wiser than I was before. These
men are not the teachers towards whose
pupils I instinctively turn; on the contrary, I
look on their devoted adherents with suspicion.

Again, Maeterlinck, it seems, is only thirty-
five years old. Now, true genius cannot so
soon be recognized. If a man of thirty-five
can get such admiration he is probably a very

good man, but he is not one of those who will
redeem Israel; and at my age I turn to these
alone or, at any rate, to such as I believe to
be these alone.   (1897.)

And here is Butler trying to judge himself:

THE ULTIMATE EFFECT OF MY BOOKS.   Who
can soberly foretell what, if any, it will be?
But, setting sobriety on one side, I have sometimes thought that it may be more considerable
than I suppose.   Certainly nothing can be
less considerable than the effect at present.
(1899.)

Corroborative evidence is forthcoming that
Butler, in dealing with the Iliad and the Odyssey,
was very much in earnest:

I should be sorry to think that I had said a
syllable upon either poem without having
considered it anxiously to the very utmost of
my power.

Erewhon was brought out in a new edition in
1901, along with *Erewhon Revisited*, and it is
pleasant to find Butler recording in his notebook:

In the course of the morning I went up into
the town [Shrewsbury] to look at the papers
and found, to my surprise, the excellent review
of *Erewhon* and *Erewhon Revisited* in *The Times*,
October 9th (on which day the books were

published), and also the hardly less excellent review in the *Daily Chronicle*.

In November, 1901, there appeared a book called *What's What* by Harry Quilter. He it was who had founded and edited *The Universal Review* in which Butler's articles had appeared. This queer hotch-potch of alphabetically arranged information contained, between " Butchers " and " Butter," articles on *Samuel Butler and his Work*, *Samuel Butler : " Quis Desiderio,"* *Samuel Butler : His Museum Grievance* and *Samuel Butler: his Odyssey Theory*. The first article opened as follows:

An author of distinguished reputation who has been before the public for nearly two score years, who is known as a wit, a thinker, a scholar and an artist, and yet who has never made a halfpenny out of any of his books ; is not this an anomalous person ? Yet such is literally the case with Mr. Samuel Butler, the author of the celebrated *Erewhon*, a book which, though published thirty years since, still remains the best imaginative satire on the Coming Race, and incidentally on existing institutions, which has yet been written. If Mr. Butler's reputation is anomalous, he is himself one of the strangest men we have ever

met. Exceptionally kind in heart, curiously
obstinate, and good humouredly prejudiced;
inscrutable in a laughing way; absolutely
careless of public opinion, full of quaint fancies
in art and literature, and instinct with a form
of wit entirely his own.

The last article ended as follows:

It is almost sufficient for a belief to be held
by the vulgar for it to be *anathema maranatha* in
Butler's eyes. This comes out especially in
The Fair Haven, a book which gave intense
offence to the orthodox. He is, indeed, one
of those personalities which find no adequate
expression in modern life. He shuns advertisement; he even loathes publicity, has a
scorn for compromise and affectation in be-
haviour; and he lived, when we first knew him,
and probably does still, the queerest hermit-like
life in an old Inn of Court, attended only by a
boy called Alfred, who was at once servant,
friend and butt for his master's good-humoured
pleasantries. Butler used to tell with great
delight the story of having left this youth to
catalogue some photographs taken by his
master on a foreign trip, and how he gave to
each of them in which he had been introduced as a foreground figure, his own name,
followed by that of the famous place—

" Alfred on the field of Waterloo," " Alfred
at the falls of the Rhine," etc. As a last word
Samuel Butler is one of the men to whom the
world has never done justice, and never understood: a wit, scholar, thinker, and chivalric
gentleman; a kind, staunch friend, and, like
Fuzzy-Wuzzy, " a first-rate fighting man."

Butler was very angry with Quilter and his
articles—much angrier than there was any reason
to be. It made him write in his note-book some
notes about Alfred, among which was this:

> I am prouder of having received and trea-
> sured these scraps of Alfred's than I am of all
> my books put together.

In 1902 appeared in *The Athenaeum* Butler's
fine sonnet beginning " Not on sad Stygian
shore."

Going over to the continent in that year, he
met on the boat a man who told him that
Eustathius, the earliest commentator on Homer
in Christian times, circa 900–1100, says that
Homer took much of his poems from a poem
written by a woman, which was preserved in the
temple of Memphis in Egypt. In Rome Butler
looked up the passage:

> 'Tis said that one Naucrates has recorded
> how a woman of Memphis, named Phantasia,

a teacher of philosophy, daughter of Nichar-
chus, composed the stories of the war before
Ilium and the wanderings of Ulysses, and
placed the books in the temple of Hephaestus
at Memphis.   Thereon Homer came there and
having obtained copies of the originals wrote
the Iliad and the Odyssey.   Some say that
either he was an Egyptian born or travelled in
Egypt and taught the people there.

While abroad, Butler was taken ill.   Of his
sister Harriet, Mrs. Garnett, who wrote her book,
Samuel Butler and his Family Relations, to vindicate
the family, says:

> To this devout and tender-hearted sister the
> estrangement was anguish, especially when the
> last scene arrived.   Misunderstandings per-
> sisted to the end.   When Butler was taken ill
> abroad, the yacht of one of Harriet's nephews
> by marriage was lying off the coast. . . .

and then she adds the passage, quoted above,
telling how Harriet, for fear of contamination
of the nephew, did not allow him to know
of Butler's need.   The illness terminated in
Butler's death.

LAST NOTEBOOKS

Butler's sixth and last volume of MS. notes
ended in March, 1902.   In it we find him saying:

I think I am a Unitarian now, but don't
know and won't say; as for the Trinity I
cannot make head or tail of it, and feel in-
clined to agree with a negro who was heard in
church here the other day repeating the
Athanasian Creed: " The Father impossible,
the Son impossible, and the Holy Ghost
impossible. And yet there are not three
impossibles, but one impossible." Professor
Sale, when I read him this in MS., told me it
was not quite accurate; he was present in
church and heard the nigger say " uncomfortable."

As Mr. Farrington so admirably said, Butler
had a mind to which natural diamonds stuck, and
here is one:

A VERY SMALL FRAGMENT OF DISCOURSE
FROM MY DEAR GOOD LAUNDRESS, MRS. CATHIE.
It was the stairs done it, and yet them houses
in York Street have got some good rooms in
them—or else, he being a doctor you'ld have
thought he'd have had the water laid on, but
no, and he must have his shower bath, and all
the time I kept dressing her finger, but that
was before I come there. It was the very
first money I ever earned, and I had finished
the dress, but while I was doing the trimmings
I ran a needle into my thumb and then I got a

bit of paint into the wound, and you can see, sir, I had three pieces of the bone took out, and the doctor, he says, "You must have that thumb cut off." "O dear me no, sir," says I, "no such thing." "But you must," says he. "The idea of the thing," says I, "and I with my living to get." Anyway them stairs brought on the dyspepsia and the indigestion, and he says to me, "Now who is it that has been dressing your thumb?" "Why," says I, "I dressed it myself," for I washed it three or four times a day in loo warm water and he says, "I will give it another week but if you don't get that thumb better by then, you will very likely lose your hand." Well, her finger got worse and worse from the moment I left off dressing it. "Why don't you keep your finger cleaner?" says he, "who is dressing it for you now?" "Why, I dress it myself," says she. I never see her for a good many years, but she went somewhere Norwich way and when I did see her I see she had lost her finger after all—and all because she did not keep it clean enough. So then he took to bringing up the water himself. "It will do me good," says he, and he used to bring canful after canful up them stairs for some days and then he had the water laid on. But no more nursing says I for me, I'd rather live by my needle.

Here is another diamond that Butler's mind held fast:

> CHILDREN IN THE MAIENTHAL. They have a pretty habit—at least some of them—of kissing the inside of their right hand before shaking hands with me. They put, as it were, a kiss under their hand before it touches mine.

SELECTIONS FROM JONES'S SELECTIONS FROM BUTLER'S NOTEBOOKS

In 1912 Jones published his selections from Butler's notebooks, and as these are in no chronological order, I give here those that seem to me most significant:

> A proof of a higher and better world is that so many come among us showing instinctive and ineradicable familiarity with a state of things which has no counterpart here, and cannot therefore have been acquired here. From such a world we come, every one of us, but some seem to have a more living recollection of it than others. Perfect recollection of it no man can have, for to put on flesh is to have all one's other memories jarred beyond power of conscious recognition.

Following this are some notes on genius, including his own:

The greatest poets never write poetry. The Homers and Shakespeares are not the greatest—they are only the greatest that we can know.   And so with Handel among musicians. For the highest poetry, whether in music or literature, is ineffable—it must be felt from one person to another, it cannot be articulated.[1]

The world will, in the end, follow only those who have despised as well as served it.

Inspiration is never genuine if it is known as inspiration at the time.   True inspiration always steals on a person; its importance not being recognized for some time.   So men of genius always escape their own immediate belongings, and indeed generally their own age.

I could not keep myself going at all if I

---

[1] Cp. Keats : " What I heard a little time ago Taylor observe with respect to Socrates may be said of Jesus—that he was so great a man that though he transmitted no writing of his own to posterity, we have his Mind and his sayings and his greatness handed on to us by others. . . . That will be one of the grandeurs of immortality—the only commerce between spirits will be by their intelligence of each other—when they will completely understand each other; " also Rupert Brooke:

> We'll . . . . . .
> Think each in each, immediately wise;
> . . . . . . hear, know, and say
> What this tumultuous body now denies;
> And feel. . . . . .
> And see, no longer blinded by our eyes.

did not believe that I was likely to inherit a good average three score years and ten of immortality.

There is no *mot d'ordre* that can keep a man permanently down if he is as intent on winning lasting good name as I have been. If I had played for immediate popularity I think I could have won it. Having played for lasting credit, I doubt not that it will in the end be given me.

Once when Butler made a fine remark to a friend, the latter said that he wished it had been in the poets.

I looked at him. " Ballard," I said, " I also am ' the poets.' "

My most intimate friends [Butler writes in another note] are men of more insight, quicker wit, more playful fancy and, in all ways, abler men than I am, but you will find ten of them for one of me. I note what they say, think it over, adapt it, and give it permanent form. They throw good things off like sparks; I collect them and turn them into warmth. But I could not do this if I did not sometimes throw out a spark or two myself.

There are one or two notes which are remarkable anticipations of conclusions that scientists have come to:

Matter and motion are functions one of another.

The only true atom which cannot be sub-divided and cut in half is the universe. The universe is the smallest piece of indivisible matter which our minds can conceive.

Compare with this Jeans's, " If we are asked how much room an electron takes up, perhaps the best answer is that it takes up the whole of space."

All the most essential and thinking part of thought is done without consciousness.

Our thought of a thing is in reality an exceedingly weak dilution of the actual thing itself.

This doctrine was subsequently enunciated in the philosophical theory of neo-realism.

Artistic forms are only evidences of an internal invisible emotion that can be felt but never fully expressed.

In the working out of a work of art, what is essential is that the artist should have begun with the most important point and added each subsequent feature in due order of importance.

Bearing in mind the shortness of life and the complexity of affairs, it stands to reason that we owe most to him who packs our trunks for us, so to speak, most intelligently, neither omitting what we are likely to want, nor including what we can dispense with, and who, at the same time, arranges things so that they will travel most safely and be got at most conveniently.

If a man never writes without thinking how he shall best serve good causes and damage bad ones, then he is a genuine man of letters. If in addition to this he succeeds in making his manner attractive, he will become a classic.

Speaking the truth, even if it is to be recorded only in a private notebook, requires more courage than most people possess. How many would have the courage to say:

> Money losses are the worst, loss of health the next worst, and loss of reputation comes in a bad third.

Anon we find him saying:

> A wound in the solicitor is a very serious thing, and many a man has died from failure of his bank's action.

He tells how a man recommended *Alps and Sanctuaries* to him:

> It would be very like me to have blurted it all out and given him to understand how fortunate he had been in meeting me; this would have been so fatally like me that the chances are ten to one that I did it.

Butler's ideals included "reticence and the healthy, graceful, normal movements of a man of birth and education"; and they also included the ethic expressed in "Surely one can laugh at a person and adore him at the same time."

In the art of life, Butler maintained that "quickness in seeing, as in everything else, comes from long sustained effort after *rightness* and comes unsought. It never comes from effort after quickness." In education the great secret is apprenticeship: "When people can sell a pupil's work, they will teach the pupil all they know and will see that he learns it." The real artist in life is he "who is so much at home with it as to be able to dissociate the permanent and the essential from the accidental which may be here to-day and gone to-morrow." The other sort of practitioners are like preachers who do not really believe their doctrine: "In a way the preachers believe what they preach, but it is as men who have taken a bad £10 note and refuse to look at the evidence that makes for its badness."

I have noted two passages in particular in these *Notebooks* for their literary quality. In the one Butler is speaking of this life as "a dawn preceding the sunrise" and he says, "True, there was a little stir—a little abiding of shepherds in the fields, keeping watch over their flocks by

night—a little buzzing in knots of men waiting
to be hired before the daybreak. . . . " In the
other he speaks of that " solemn, old-world
feeling, as though we had stumbled unexpectedly
on some holy, peaceful survivors of an age long
gone by, when the struggle was not so fierce and
the world was a sweeter, happier place than we
now find it."

When we look back on the latter part of
Butler's life, we can see that from his father's
death, Butler's relief and revitalization were
great. His grandfather did not disappoint him,
nor Alfred, nor Hans. His insight and creative
power were such that, says Mrs. Stillman, he was
able to create the young girl of genius whom he
discovered in the Odyssey and the woman of the
world as Yram in *Erewhon Revisited*.[1]

This revitalization of Butler can be seen in the
photographs reproduced in the late Mr. Bartholomew's *Butleriana* dating from March, 1888, and
from 1890 respectively. In the former Butler is
in profundis, suffering, a stoic ; in the latter his
face is rounded, almost jovial (although with the
subliminal sadness that is always there, the
expression of spirit crucified in matter), his beard
trimmed to a point.

[1] *Samuel Butler*, p. 293.

In 1903 *The Way of All Flesh* was published on the consent of Mr. Streatfeild, Butler's literary executor, in spite of the fact that Butler's sisters were still living.

Let us now try to see Butler in his manner as he was. His standard of living was of the very simplest. He did " chores " for himself such as cooking his own breakfast and fetching water every day. He said it was good for him to have a change of occupation. " This," says Jones, " was partly the fact, but the real reason was that he shrank from inconveniencing anybody: he always paid more than was necessary when anything was done for him and was not happy then unless he did some of the work himself."

Mr. Yeats, with deep insight, has pointed out in connexion with Butler that an affectionate mother wants her children to be good rather less than she wants them to be happy. Love covers a multitude of sins. The maternal in Butler took this view. Therefore a like charity ought to be extended to him, and it has not been altogether lacking. On Butler's death, Canon McCormick wrote of him to *The Times*:

Samuel Butler, I fancy, lived too much alone. We must not altogether judge him as we would other men. But, say the best or the worst of him, I am myself satisfied that he was far better than what might be called his creed; and, coupled with unique intellectual powers, there was childlike simplicity and a heart full of the warmest and most constant affection for his friends.

The key to the paradox of Butler—his strong attractive and strong repellent power—is that he was abnormally sensitive. He learnt through bitter experience how untrustworthy conventions are, and he knew he was not getting justice while much inferior men were being lauded to the skies. " Butler," says Jones, " was always nervous and diffident about his own manners and appearance unless he was interested in the company or the conversation, and then he forgot everything else. This wore off to a certain extent as he grew older, but to the last he used to make bread pills at a dinner party." " He was seldom at his best with a celebrated man. He was not successful himself, and had a sub-aggressive feeling that a celebrated man probably did not deserve his celebrity; if he did deserve it, let him prove it. Possibly the celebrity felt, as I did, that Butler was not merely waiting for the production of the proofs, but was more than half prepared to find them unconvincing. If so, it is easy to understand why these meetings were sometimes chilly."

" Earnestness was his greatest danger, but if he did not quite overcome it (as, indeed, who can? it is the last enemy that shall be subdued), he managed to veil it with a fair amount of success." Butler was thinking of himself when he wrote this of Beaconsfield. He knew that " a little levity will save many a good heavy thing from sinking." Sometimes he risked being misunderstood, but he was writing neither for those who do not think over what they read, nor for those who are easily thrown off their balance, nor for those who cannot penetrate—he was writing in the hope of finding people likeminded to himself. The truth is that what was characteristic of Butler was that in him sincerity was carried to a phenomenally high degree.

Jones insists that the kind of man Butler liked was not necessarily one who agreed with him in the matters at issue but one who was a voice and not an echo—although it must be confessed that to a man of Butler's type it is very difficult not to prefer those agreeing on important matters at issue. Sir William Phipson Beale, Q.C., a friend of Butler, said to Jones, " People misunderstood Butler: he did not want praise, he wanted sympathy," and with this Jones agreed. Mr. Fuller Maitland wrote of Butler: " My affection for him would have led me to accept any theory he formed, to agree with him in his interpretation of Shakespeare's sonnets, to consider Handel the greatest of all composers, to hail Tabachetti as a great sculptor, and to damn to perdition Darwin and all his descendants. . . . I am not sure that Festing Jones, in the famous biography of his friend, has quite conveyed the elfin humorist, the Puckish love of mischief, or the irresistible charm of Butler."[1] Festing Jones wrote "To me he was the dearest, kindest, most considerate friend that any man ever had. He was never selfish or egoistic, nor was there ever anything that required explanation." The Revd. Cuthbert Creighton, son of Bishop Creighton, expressed the vision which reveals the solution of the paradox of Butler:

I can see shining, or perhaps I ought rather to say twinkling, through his pages the personality of a man of rare lovable character, one who, though this may sound an unexpected note on which to end and though the idea would have brought an incredulous smile to his lips, always seems to me to have had in him something of what I conceive to be saintliness.

Of Butler surely may be said what has been said of another: "It has been recognized that he did

_____
[1] *A Door-keeper of Music*, pp. 265-6.

great and splendid things far outweighing his mistakes—things so great that it is wholly unnecessary to deify him; that his character was in essence one of gold, tested in such fires that we need not try to conceal the clinging fragments of clay."[1] But most people would agree that if God exists and His will is known, the highest life is in *doing* His will. Now the difference between the thought of most orthodox people and Butler's is parallel to that between being dependent on unearned increment and working for one's living.[2] It is also indicated in the false perspective that comes from attention to small facts in blindness to the spirit that gives them their significance. Butler himself expressed it, among many expressions of it, in a note in one of his notebooks:

THE HIGHER RULES OF LIFE

They transcend all language; they cannot be gotten by speech, neither shall logic be weighed for the price thereof; they have their being in the fear of the Lord and the departing from evil, without even knowing in words what the Lord is, nor the fear of the Lord, nor yet evil.

But the working out, the application of these rules in life, as was largely done by Butler, has been magnificently described in a leader in *The Times*:

---

[1] *The Times*, December 5, 1932.
[2] Kingsmill, *After Puritanism*, p. 104.

O

" The greater simplicity is based, not on negation, but on knowledge and strength. Positive and powerful, the greater simplicity can come only of close scrutiny of the facts of life and deliberate reduction of their chaotic variety to form and order. From that process emerge principles, beliefs and aims, to which all else is made subordinate and subsidiary. The resultant simplification has much of the charm of its childish prototype but escapes its obvious deficiencies. Its tenuity is the spareness of the trained athlete, not the lank meagreness of immaturity. Simplicity of this kind is not reached but by prayer and fasting. The man who attains to it holds the clue to the labyrinth of a complicated world. Even physically it guides him along the sane path between excess and atrophy. Mentally he wields canons and judgments which cleave a straight way through wordiness and irrelevancy. Morally, though he must be watchful to the end, he ceases to be the field of a wildly swaying conflict. It is easy to see what strength is added to a man so furnished. His speech is plain and lucid. Those who listen to him embrace no cloud of parentheses and reservations: he can afford to leave the exuberance of oratory and the windings of subtlety to others. His actions are direct and unhesitating. He is not drawn astray on side issues; he is aware of them, but aware also of their lower place in the order of importance. He develops an X-ray mind, which can pierce the outer opacities and see to the heart of things. His personality precipitates obscurities and flows clear and bright.   Such simplicity is a talisman which, when things go well with him, keeps the eye of the simple man " unruined 'mid the fierce and flashing splendour," and no less, when things go ill, holds his heart unshaken by mishap.   He is, more than any other, master of himself and of his fate.   By virtue of that greater simplicity a man may still find the key to the gate of his kingdom by becoming even as a little child."

As is most fitting, it was Festing Jones who wrote the ultimate truth about Butler:

Nothing ever shook his belief that if a man loves God, he cannot come to much harm. We may not always know what is meant by God, and things may not always work together for the particular good we desire; but there is " a something as yet but dimly known that makes right right and wrong wrong," and no man can ultimately fail who obeys the dictates of that voice which we can all hear if we will but listen.   But he must obey without regard to theological dogmas or social conventions; he must never allow mistakes to dishearten him—mistakes made in good faith will teach him more than anything else; and he must never grow weary of taking pains.

INDEXES

1. The Writings of Samuel Butler.

2. General